Praise for Fourteen Hills

"Beautifully designed, impeccably edited, *Fourteen Hills*
is one of those handful of literary journals doing the important
work of keeping American writing alive and new."
George Saunders, author of *In Persuasion Nation*

"The journal is something of a collage itself, boasting a variety
of talented writers from San Francisco and around the world."
Jennifer Gomoll, *NewPages.com*

"[*Fourteen Hills*] blends the traditional litmag with
experimental writing in a slick, well-produced journal."
Todd Dayton, *MetroACTIVE*

"Smart, quirky, literate—every piece in this journal gives
the reader a juicy nugget to sink their teeth into, and
something meaty that sticks to the mind's ribs."
David Henry Sterry, author of *Chicken*

Fourteen Hills

Vol. 17 No. 1

2011

The San Francisco State
University Review

Acknowledgements.

Fourteen Hills would like to thank the following for help and support in putting this issue together:

Maxine Chernoff
Barbara Eaton
DJ Martin Hodge
D.W. Lichtenberg
Annemarie Munn
San Francisco Motorcycle Club

Jennifer Daly
Christopher Hayter
Jessica Kaihoi
Jason Lujick
Peter Orner

Fourteen Hills would like to thank the following businesses and individuals for their generous donations to our fundraising events:

222 Hyde, Alba Fiore, Andrew Kornblatt, Annemarie Munn, Bi-Rite Creamery, Ethos Coffee, Fiftyseven-Thirtythree, Front Porch, Green Apple Books, Ink Press, Internos, Wine Café, Mercury Café, Mocha 101, Modern Times Bookstore, Omnibucket, Pegasus Books, Periscope Cellars Winery, The Poetry Center & American Poetry Archives, Red Vic Movie House.

Credits.

Book Layout and Design: Hollie Hardy, Stephen Rosenshein, and Annemarie Munn
Cover and Art Design: S.B. Stokes and Hollie Hardy
Copy Editors: Hollie Hardy, Leanne Milway, Don Menn, and Stephen Rosenshein
Cover Artwork: Damon Soule. "Sequenced Events" mixed media 16" x 20"

Distribution.

Small Press Distribution, Berkeley, California / www.spdbooks.org
Ubiquity Distributors, Inc., Brooklyn, New York / www.ubiquitymags.com

ISSN: 1085-4576
ISBN: 978-1-889292-50-2

Fourteen Hills is published by the Creative Writing Department at San Francisco State University, with the support of the Instructionally Related Activities Fund.

Fourteen Hills

Vol. 17 No. 1

2011

Hollie Hardy
Editor-in-Chief

Leanne Milway
Managing Editor

Stephen Rosenshein
Poetry Editor

Lori Savageau
Fiction Editor

S.B. Stokes
Assistant Poetry Editor

Michael Urquidez
Fiction Editor

Matthew DeCoster
Editorial Intern

Scott Lambridis
Non-Fiction Editor

Matthew Clark Davison
Faculty Advisor

Editorial Staff

Benjamin Black · Rose Booker · Stephanie Doeing

Erica Eller · Adam Hofbauer · Jason Johnson

Kelly McNerney · Don Menn · Chani Mooring

Rod Roland · Matthew Sherling · Zofia Turchin

Phillip Van Sant · Sandra Wassilie

Fourteen Hills is published twice yearly in San Francisco, California

Subscriptions:
Individual – One year for $15. Two years for $28.
Institutional – One year for $17. Two years for $32.
Single issues $9.

Submissions should be accompanied by a self-addressed, stamped envelope. We have a rolling submissions policy, so you may submit at any time, but the cutoff for inclusion in our issue is August 1 for the Fall issue; January 1 for the Spring issue. All correspondence should be addressed to the appropriate editor at Fourteen Hills, c/o the Creative Writing Department, San Francisco State University, 1600 Holloway Ave., San Francisco, CA 94132. Fourteen Hills does not accept unsolicited electronic submissions.

www.14hills.net

Contents.

Fourteen Hills

Brian Boitano Eighties

from The Eighties, a Brief Primer

Michael Reid Busk

In 1989, Brian Boitano was elected President of the Eighties. Although the yearlong position was mostly honorary, it came with a few perks: a new and rust-free Yugo, at least one guaranteed appearance on *The Arsenio Hall Show*, many Adidas track suits, one intern/assistant, chosen from an enormous pool of applicants, all rising seniors at one of the Seven Sisters schools, and a two-bedroom split-level in Cleveland, to be used as a headquarters for the president's initiatives.

Being the last year of what was even then understood to be an unprecedentedly glorious decade, the campaigning was fierce. Although not technically American, Bono was running for a third term (having already been elected in 1983 and 1985), but many believed he was becoming too theatrical and self-aggrandizing (see *African Benefit Concert Eighties*). Rural areas were strong in their support of Kris Kristofferson, but his campaign was disorganized and, to this day it isn't clear if he ever knew he was running. A postman from Topeka who could moonwalk while reciting *Hamlet* enjoyed a brief spike of popularity, but when it became clear his platform was nothing but postal reform and a mandatory return to the spellings and grammatical norms of Elizabethan English, his support dissolved. The Boitano campaign— ruthlessly efficient, unswervingly centrist—proved the race is not always to the swift, nor to Irish rock stars who wear sunglasses at night.

Within minutes of Boitano's swearing-in on a Calvin Klein coffee table book, lakes and ponds throughout the states began to freeze of their own accord; citizens found their limbs had acquired the fluid elegance of streamers at the opening ceremonies of the Olympics (see *Olympics Eighties*); pants shrunk a few sizes and pleats flew unstitched; for the first time, the word *axel* was more frequently uttered than the word *axle*; parents began judging the skill and grace of their children's motions by raising white placards imprinted with a number on the six-point scale.

In step with the times, the Boitano administration was a major proponent of charter schools, in particular those emphasizing winter sports and the dance arts. The students of such schools received clothing gratis that year from the Boitano administration's two largest donors: the American Association of Spandex Manufacturers, and the sequin industry. The reception to those uniforms was mixed.

Throughout the year, Boitano gave lectures across the nation explaining the benefits of low-impact cardio, the evils of Communism (see *Russian Eighties, Olympics Eighties*), and touting his favorite recipes: Yam Delite and Bacon Cake. However, he grew fond of his adopted city of Cleveland, and could often be found touring the city in his rust-free Yugo, stopping regularly to ask residents how they thought the Eighties might be improved and volunteering to sign any piece of paper, clothing, or body part they might have handy with a puffy paint pen. Everyone told him they were happy to be more elegant, leaping and spinning for no reason but the joy of it, and they all agreed that pleats were a bad idea, wondering how they could have worn them for so long. For years, Cleveland natives could be immediately identified by the huge, looping puffy paint Bs clinging to the items of clothing they refused to wash even after the end of Boitano's term, which of course coincided with the end of the decade. He left office just as Dick Clark wished America a Happy New Year, packing up his baking pans and sequined boleros, trailing his gold medal over the split-level's mantle, kissing his intern Kelsey on both cheeks, and locking the door behind himself.

Almost immediately, at gatherings throughout the country, guests noticed their motions grew blocky and stiff-jointed, and they drove home over bridges that spanned thawing bodies of water to houses with closets full again of pleated pants that seemed suddenly appealing. Boitano himself was never seen again, although occasionally, deep in the heart of a particularly frigid Ohio winter, Cleveland natives still claim to see a man clad in a tight black leotard skating in great serpentine curls over the frozen face of Lake Erie, pirouetting into the low sky in a marvelous series of triple axels.

Remnants

Renee Emerson

A pack of unsent letters. His mother's penmanship her best
quality, flourished and curled where her words would not.

Dated by the yellow tinge, a strand of hair caught in a fold,
holes burnt through from writing with a cigarette in one hand,

pen in the other. Assortment of stains—coffee, make-up, ash.
Letters folded and refolded, creasing out words.

On the back of an unpaid bill: "I read your snake poem today, it was
delightful" and on the hotel napkin— "I know you talk a lot. I've heard

you." These were from a long time ago, worn thin.
Exposed to sunlight, he could see through them, like clean water.

My Sister Calls to Tell Me

Renee Emerson

She's going to be a radiologist.
She explains it has nothing to do with radio,
although I like to picture her, ear to the dial,
twisting it slowly, a thief at a safe, tracing
the tenors back to that ache we all feel.

August. An awkward month.
A month where I say "let's spend the day outdoors"
in our overgrown yard, in mosquitoes,
in the hazed sun, the cicada buzz.

We spend the day indoors instead,
polishing minor victories
our thoughts rub over, again and again,

like our cats curve their bodies
against our legs in the yard, lonely

for us, if they can feel
like we can feel, banished,
coats laced with fleas.

They don't know any better. Some would say
the same about us, listening close to the static.

Sancho's World

Molly Prentiss

Today the world reminded me of the world. No one avoided anyone, and those who avoided things only avoided themselves. All gazes: turned outward. All feet: aimed forward. B., my wife, was busy catering a wedding, so I catered to myself. I catered to the deep need I have for discovering things by way of walking. I stepped into the street without B., which was a novel way for me to step into the street.

Sancho Street was humming. Or rather, Sancho was humming. Sancho lived on Sancho Street. Or rather, we called the street Sancho Street because of Sancho. Sancho's hum lifted off of the ground like a motorized airplane. I held the remote control to that airplane; when I stepped toward Sancho his hum would dip down deep and when I stepped back it would level again. Sancho wore a moustache, was homeless, and had a voice like nice wind. He had made love to B. on occasions when I was out of town. I knew this because pieces of his voice were always left in the apartment.

I patted Sancho on the back and gave him a coin. I turned left on Calle Matamoros. I didn't want to be excluded from Calle Matamoros, and you had to get there before eleven to be included. It was 10:52. I had made it to the happening. Or rather, they hadn't made anything happen yet. The auctioneer had not started auctioning. The club boys were still paddling around drinking red beer. In the relative quiet, I could still hear Sancho's humming, weaving through the club boys and their beer voices. Then the auction started. The auctioneer's voice was a list, and he was checking everything off. He sold a bird in a cage, and then a set of ancient dolls that fit eagerly inside of each other. He auctioned off a package that included two cars and a book. The book was written in a Slavic language that I couldn't understand. A club boy—wearing red— bought the package. He yelled something in Russian. Or rather, Russian yelled its way out of him. It was marvelous what he yelled. He yelled: I only wanted the book! The book is worth a hundred cars!

I wanted to be included in being included, so I bought something from the auctioneer. What I bought was a gift for B. It was a world. Or rather, it was the world condensed into a world. It was a globe. The Russian club boy cheered me on. He bounded up to me and spun the globe. Then he spun out of control. He splashed his red beer around like blood. He danced Slavicly. I quickly left Calle Matamoros with my globe, spinning away from him and his spinning.

Everybody loved my globe. It attracted audiences of all kinds, especially kids, who yanked their mothers' hands and begged to have a spin. Italian mothers begged me with their eyes. "Please," the mothers said, "let my kid spin your globe. Just this once. If you don't let my kid spin your globe he will be cranky while I am cooking ravioli, and his tears will get into the pasta water. Then his dad will get home and say the pasta is too salty, turn away from me in bed. His dad will say *Cazzo! Cosa fai?* And we will never have sex again, if you do not let my kid spin your globe." So of course, I let them. Their fat fingers landed on any country. They always said, "So this is where I was meant to go."

I held my globe close, wiped the grease from Argentina. Noticed a smudge of something on Rwanda; dabbed my finger on it. Tasted it. Wondered if I was meant to go there. Or there. Or there. I turned on one foot away from the mothers and kids. Turned a corner somewhere. Stopped. I held the globe close, kissed New York, said out loud, "Nothing's going to get in my way."

A Chinese woman with many plastic bags got in my way. The plastic bags were as pink as her bonnet. Or rather, her bonnet—a scarf really—was as pink as a sunset. This pink color reminded me of B.'s ears when she was embarrassed. Thinking about B.'s ears, I grew embarrassed. I used the globe to cover my crotch. I smiled at the Chinese lady. She pulled a tangerine from her pink bag, held it up next to my globe, and laughed. "All the same," she said in Chinese. "It is all the same."

I went to the waterfront. The water swayed bashfully in front of the waterfront. Or rather, the water seemed to be getting undressed. It was coming forward and revealing something indecent, then retreating again. Again I held the globe in front of my crotch. The water sounded like B. when she slept, and when B. slept, I always got embarrassed. Something about her body being a body, and being so close to my own body. Something about bodies being made of water, the way they rippled. Then a body appeared in a body suit, kind of baggy. The baggy suit covered the whole body, even the eyes. The body bag came toward me.

"Hey," the body bag said, sticking out a wet finger. "Isn't that Sancho's globe?" He sounded territorial. Or rather, he sounded like he was made of territory.

"It's an auction globe," I said.

"Calle Matamoros?" The body bag said.

"Yes," I said.

At this the body bag loosened, pulled the cover down from his face. It hung around his neck like a skin. "Cool, bro," the body under the body bag said, as if I were his brother suddenly, as if Calle Matamoros was a club, as if because I had danced with the club boys, I was part of that club. But why had he called it Sancho's globe? How did the body bag guy know Sancho, and if this was Sancho's globe, how did Sancho get his hands on something so beautiful, so expensive and marvelous?

I turned away from the body bag. I waved to him from behind my back. I ran back to Sancho Street, the world bouncing with me as I ran. Sancho was still sitting inside of his moustache. I squatted down in front of him, my globe clutched to my chest.

Something in Sancho changed when I squatted. I was bending at the knees, but Sancho was bending at the brain. Or rather, his eyes were bending like sadness.

"What's wrong, Sancho?" I asked.

"That globe belongs to B.," he said.

"Yes! I bought it for her. It is a gift."

"It was a gift," Sancho said.

"It *is* a gift!" I said. I bought it at the auction!

"I *made* that globe," Sancho said.

I was silent, my hands stiffening around the earth.

"For B.," Sancho said.

I was silent, my hands stiffening around the earth.

"She got rid of the world I made for her," Sancho said sadly.

Now I was clenching my teeth. I imagined Sancho in the apartment with his shoes off; I imagined Sancho making the globe with paper mache, spitting on countries to make them shine; I imagined Sancho dancing Slavicly, fucking an Italian mother, helping the Chinese with their plastic bags. I imagined Sancho and B. at the waterfront, undressing for each other, spinning with fireflies. There would be fireflies for them, wouldn't there? There would be a moon, wouldn't there?! The man in the body bag had seen them, hadn't he? The world had seen them, hadn't it? The globe started to spin without anyone touching it. Sancho and I looked into each other's eyes. The whole world was spinning for B., and there was no sense in stopping it with our feeble hands.

&

At a wedding, in a valley between two hilltops, B. caters to a swarm of wealthy guests. She caters to their every need: their bashful blotting and their drunk dabbling. B. has catered three weddings this weekend, and her feet are tired, clumped up like hard little loaves in her clogs. This particular wedding is a traditional Indian wedding, and she has been asked to wear henna on her hands and arms. The henna moves up her fingers and tickles her forearms. She understands that it is meant to be beautiful, but she does not like the way it attracts attention to her hands, like a fly in the room, catching her eye every so often, interrupting. In a portable bathroom with a plastic sink she scrubs at her hands with almond scented soap, until her skin turns raw, and the ornate markings glow red at the edges.

When she steps outside again, the guests are leaving the valley. They are leaving in two directions: the women over one hilltop, the men over the other. They are wearing brightly colored clothes and cloth, and look like petals scattering over the green hills. B. thinks of what will happen when she goes home to her apartment. Her apartment that still smells like Sancho, a mix of spicy food and paper mache—all of the things he *made* for her. She will use three keys to unlock the door, set down her bags, full of leftover daal, and chutney, and almond flavored cookies, and go immediately to the cabinet above the refrigerator. She will pull out a glass jar with a tin lid, open the lid and place the mouth of the jar to the shell of her ear, and listen for Sancho's humming. Her husband will come into the kitchen with sleepy eyes, wrap his hard arms around her. He will pull the jar away from her ear, kiss her neck, and whisper: *I have something for you.*

After 15 Years, My Wife Said Thank You And I'm Sorry

Charlotte Pence

Nothing lasts, we know, so why do I lift
The box turtle from the middle of the road
To the side where crab grass pocks asphalt crumbs?
Picking it up, I feel the tight-fisted weight
Of some creature shrunken inside, desperate
To be set down. I hold it away from my chest
As if I don't want to touch it, trace
Its nail-smooth underside halved by a seam
As rough as a re-scabbed wound. The longer I stand,
Unsure of what to do, the longer I give the turtle
That dizzying sense of no control. I know that feeling
As sure as I know the sound of hard-soled shoes
Grinding roadside gravel. *Set it down. Set
It down.* Here—or there—almost doesn't matter.

Today, the Role of Bruce Willis Will Be Played by My Dad...

Jason Bayani

Sitting around the breakfast nook; my mother; carefully folding into herself; hands softening around the undone patchwork resting on her palms. My father's tongue: a blunt device made heavier by the weight of his native dialect. He yelled at her, *Bakit!?* Why? Why can't you do these simple things I tell you to do? English words are unable to hold my father's passion. Maybe this is why my mother chose to fall out of language when she asks him, *Do you want to hit me?* He collapsed into a hard pause; counterbalanced by a man's stubborn need to be the right one—to win. *No,* he told her, his jaw tightening to a pulse—walking away, her face reduced to dull pallor.

Later that day he took us to the movies and let me choose. I leveraged the morning's incident towards a movie with an R rating. Two hours into watching it: Bruce Willis gruffing his way through implausible feats of bullet dodging and populist machismo, he finds his wife (assumed dead) in the middle of a snowy airfield and acceptable man tears well up on his face as he holds her tightly in his arms. My father, sitting next to me, stumbles into a graceless attempt at wiping the tears that had begun welling up in his own eyes. The laughter my mother was carefully stifling, pistoned into a mild snort—*Umi iyak ka ba?* Are you crying, my mother asks. Resigned, he helplessly flails his arms towards the screen—*His wife,* he said, *he thought he lost his wife.*

Saluting the Magpie

Jacob M. Appel

Domestic upheaval: Our daughter, Calliope, swallows a penny. We've just celebrated her first birthday, and streamers still festoon the living room, when I hear Gillian shouting as though pirates have climbed up the fire escape. Not that pirates pose much of a threat on a balmy spring afternoon in Brooklyn, of course, but pirates are a useful shorthand for the lengthy list of unspeakable horrors that I suppose ought to flash through my mind as I fumble for the shower door and stagger down the hallway wrapped in a bath towel. Gillian has a knack for enumerating these horrors, which she does vividly whenever we drop the baby off at my mother's: feral dogs, and exposed wires, and kidnappers on the payroll of black-market adoption brokers. At the moment, none of these threats enter my thoughts. That's one of the differences between Gillian and me. What I'm actually thinking is: If Gillian keeps screaming like a crazy person, the widowed sisters living upstairs are going to complain to the landlord again. Of course, I know enough not to shout at my wife to quit screaming. In any case, she stops on her own once I've dripped my way into the kitchen, where she's bracing our red-faced Calliope on one knee and tapping the child's back with the heel of her palm.

"Thank God you're here!" Gillian cries—as though she has been awaiting my arrival for hours. "She swallowed a penny. Can you please do something?"

"Is she okay?"

"How can she possibly be okay? Jesus, Dave. She swallowed a fucking coin."

I don't know how my daughter can be okay. I'm a botanist, not a physician. But the girl is beaming from ear to ear, apparently proud of her deed. A cursory inspection of her neck reveals no unusual bulges.

I kiss Calliope's forehead. "I guess it will come out eventually," I say.

"You cannot be serious," snaps Gillian. "Nothing is happening *eventually*. All that toxic copper is leaching into her system *right now*. Not *eventually*. Am I making myself clear, Dave? My baby isn't a goddam piggybank."

Not a choice time, I realize, to explain that pennies are made primarily from zinc.

"Okay, I'll call Dr. Frey," I offer.

"Here. Take her." Gillian deposits our child in my arms. "You know exactly what Dr. Frey is going to say. She's going to say not to worry." My wife picks up the wall telephone and adds, "*This* is why we need a new doctor. If Cal swallowed a live grenade, Dr. Frey would say not to worry."

I have no opportunity to defend our pediatrician before Gillian asks the operator to put her call through to Poison Control. Meanwhile, I tickle Calliope's tummy until she giggles, so my wife's distress won't alarm her. Three hundred sixty-six days have passed since this enchanting, feral creature entered our world—we are in a leap year—and I am still dumbfounded that her entire existence is half my doing. I am grinning, and Calliope is squealing, when the other responsible party covers the telephone receiver and thrusts it into my hand.

"You talk to him," Gillian insists. "He wants to know about the penny."

I glare at her—trying to wish my eyeballs into harpoons.

A male voice with a thick Indian accent greets me at the other end of the line. "So you are telling me that your child has ingested a penny," he says. "Is that correct?"

"Yes, that is correct."

I can hear the man typing, probably one of hundreds of similar young Indian men packed into an over-airconditioned office suite or gymnasium in Hyderabad or Bangalore or wherever, fielding emergency calls from the United States on the graveyard shift. For all that I know, the man has never even *seen* an American penny.

"What kind of penny?" he asks.

"What do you mean: What *kind* of penny?" I fire back. "A penny."

"All right, sir. Do you happen to know the year of the penny?"

"No, I don't know the year of the penny."

"Thank you, sir. You are telling me you do not know the year of the penny. Do you know at which location the penny was minted?"

"Excuse me?"

"If you will please look on the front of the coin, under the date, you may see a letter D, a letter S, or no letter at all. Are you able to look at the front of the coin?"

I refuse to let myself become frustrated. The man is just doing his job. I imagine he thinks we Americans are incompetent parents for letting our daughters eat our money.

"The penny is *inside* my daughter's stomach," I explain. "So *no*, I do not know at which location it was minted."

A long pause follows. I suppose this contingency is not on the therapeutic algorithm used by outsourced Poison Control agents. The man confers with a colleague in his native language, his words fast and anxious, before returning to me.

"Very well, sir. You are telling me that the penny is inside the stomach of your daughter," he says—still ineffably polite. "Under these circumstances, I must recommend that you seek further medical assistance at a hospital."

I thank the man for his insight and hang up the phone, determined not to endure a Sunday afternoon waiting for a doctor. "Poison Control agrees with me," I inform Gillian. "Nothing to worry about. Kids swallow coins all the time."

"I could care less what Poison Control says," she answers, already bundling Calliope into her outdoor cloak. "We're going to the emergency room."

One might ask why a person phones Poison Control *at all* if one is determined to take one's daughter to the emergency room *anyway*. After eight years of dating and five of marriage, a man learns not to ponder such impenetrable mysteries. My wife's personal choices are as complex and inscrutable as the highly-prized collages she fashions from discarded grocery packaging. And will remain so. Not even love can decipher them; it can only embrace them.

I recognize that the penny episode has become my responsibility, even though the swallowing occurred on Gillian's watch. I'm so certain of what I'm in for, that the accusation, when it finally arrives, is almost reassuring.

"What were you *thinking*?" demands Gillian.

We're in the back seat of a taxi, inching up Flatbush Avenue toward the hospital.

I brace myself. "Thinking about what?"

"Who leaves pennies within reach of a one-year-old?" To add to my discomfort, Gillian leans forward and asks the turbaned cabbie, "Would *you* leave pennies within reach of a one-year old?"

"You have a very beautiful child," the driver replies with diplomacy. "You are very lucky to have such a beautiful child."

◇

The pediatric emergency room on a Sunday afternoon is enough to scare any would-be parent into permanent celibacy. Ailing children wait on mechanized cots, enduring bloody eyes and swollen limbs, while their restless siblings scamper around IV poles and beneath cardiac monitors with minimal supervision. By the time we arrive, all of the beds are occupied, so we're assigned to a gurney in a corridor opposite the triage bay. On the adjacent gurney sits a shirtless, obese boy, at the cusp of adolescence, who insists on flashing his abdominal rash to passersby.

"It's painless," he informs us while his mother visits the restroom. "I looked it up on the Internet last night and I'm pretty sure it's syphilis."

At the opposite end of the passageway, a maintenance crew labors behind a cordon of yellow signs, mopping away another patient's vomit. Gillian and I take turns singing "Bye, Baby Bunting," Calliope's favorite lullaby, for over two hours, until our daughter finally dozes off. Minutes later, the pediatric resident arrives to examine her.

The young doctor appears kind, but obviously overwhelmed. Stray papers keep falling from the pockets of her white coat. Also M&M wrappers. When she leans forward to retrieve them, tongue depressors and plastic otoscope caps tumble out of her other pocket. She smiles apologetically, but she looks as though she's on the verge of tears—a reminder of how thankful I am that I decided to study the physiology of seaweed rather than human disease.

"I'm sorry," she apologizes. "It's my first day."

"But you *are* a pediatrician?" demands Gillian.

"Actually, I'm a psychiatry intern," explains the young doctor. "We rotate through the emergency room. But we're well supervised." She touches my wife's shoulder to console her. "Now tell me what happened?"

I relate to the resident how I left my pocket change on the kitchen countertop and how Calliope transformed a penny into an *hors d'oeuvre*. "A 1997 penny, minted in Philadelphia," I speculate—for no good reason. "Manufactured primarily out of zinc."

Gillian throws me a suspicious glance. The resident nods sympathetically.

"We should get an X-ray," says the young doctor. "To make sure the coin's not lodged within her esophagus. If it's in her stomach, we'll just let it pass on through."

The resident presses gently on Calliope's belly, peers into her throat with a penlight. I could as easily have performed the same examination at home. "I don't think it's anything to worry about," she declares. "My boss may stop by to say hello and then we'll get her that X-ray. But I'm afraid it could take a little while. We're down to one machine." She looks at us nervously, as though seeking approval. "Do you have any questions or concerns?"

"What was your name?" asks Gillian.

"I'm Dr. Clampitt," replies the young doctor. "But you can call me Maia."

So we wait another four hours for an X-ray. Soon the overflow corridor is crammed to capacity and two orderlies slide another gurney between ours and the fat boy's. He shows his rash to the new patient, a four-year-old girl nursing a toothache. The child soothes her pain with cloth-wrapped ice, which melts quickly inside the crowded ER, and she keeps dispatching her bespectacled grandaunt to obtain more cubes. Later, the girl asks Gillian, "What's syphilis?" By the time they summon Calliope for her dose of unnecessary radiation, I'm ready to start swallowing coins myself.

Gillian accompanies Calliope into the X-ray suite. I purchase a cup of coffee from a vending machine and pace outside the swinging doors. An attractive brunette takes a seat on a nearby bench, and I find myself admiring her body out of the corner of my eye, until I suddenly realize that I am looking at Dr. Frey. Our pediatrician sports tight-fitting jeans and an angora sweater than emphasizes her physique. I am accustomed to seeing her in a long, sterile lab coat. Her eyes catch mine, and she greets me by name.

"My nephew tripped on a garden hose," she explains. She has accompanied her sister's son for his X-rays, hoping to speed the process. "Without the right connections," she observes, "you can wait here for days."

"I know," I reply.

I relate the afternoon's events yet again—this time revealing that the swallowing episode occurred under Gillian's supervision. I can't help thinking that, if matrimony were entirely a scientific endeavor, I'd have married someone much like Elsa Frey. Our pediatrician is even-tempered, eminently reasonable. She also enjoys gardening, I've discovered—unlike Gillian, who couldn't tell a radish from a rutabaga. And, it's only fair to acknowledge, Elsa Frey is very easy on the eyes. But romance *isn't* a scientific equation. I've been in love with Gillian since she cheated off me on a tenth grade chemistry quiz, copying the alkali metals and the noble gases, and I can't conceive of loving anybody else. When my wife returns from the X-ray suite with our daughter's tiny pink arms wrapped around her neck, she's as dazzlingly attractive as on our first date.

"Look who I found," I declare.

I feel that I've redeemed myself by producing Dr. Frey—like a magician who flubs one trick and then pulls off another—but Gillian doesn't appear impressed.

Our pediatrician instructs my wife to set Calliope on a nearby stretcher and she performs a physical examination of her own. A far more thorough workup than the psychiatry intern's cursory effort. She borrows a stethoscope from a passing medical student and has him listen to our daughter's chest as well.

"It could be absolutely nothing," she observes. "A one-time fluke. Kids like to put things in their mouths....On the other hand, it could be pica."

The only pika I know are the chinchilla-like rodents we encountered while camping in Utah, but I don't mention this.

"What's pica?" inquires Gillian.

"Some children develop cravings for non-nutritive substances," explains Dr. Frey. "Chalk. Soap. *Coins*. Nobody knows why." She cleanses the stethoscope's diaphragm with an alcohol pad and returns it to the medical student. "Pica is the Latin word for magpie. They say magpies will eat anything. Goats of the sky, they're called." The pediatrician shakes hands with Calliope, then with Gillian and me. "It's likely nothing to worry about. Just don't leave any more coins lying around the house and she should be fine....Of course, if she *does* have another episode, definitely bring her by the office."

Maia Clampitt returns with the X-ray results a few moments later. The penny has settled safely into Calliope's stomach, an opaque white crescent on a field of black. In other words, our field trip has been an utter waste of time, but I don't point this out to Gillian. In the cab, I'm actually feeling rather conciliatory toward her. It dawns upon me that we haven't spoken, in any meaningful way, since our arrival at the emergency room.

"Isn't there a nursery rhyme about magpies?" I ask to break the silence. "*One for sorrow, two for joy, three for a girl, four for a boy....*"

"What?"

"I had this British zoology professor at Yale—Dr. April—and he used the expression 'saluting the magpie' all the time, because in England a solitary magpie is bad luck, and saluting it is supposedly a way to protect yourself...to claim your own territory....But then some visiting students from Oxford told us that it's also an off-color expression for something else entirely...and now I can't think of magpies without thinking of Dr. April's pecker...."

"For God's sake, Dave," interrupts Gillian. "Your daughter nearly dies and all you can think about are nursery rhymes!"

I turn to face my wife, waiting for the next blow. I know that her anxiety has not developed in a vacuum. When Gillian was only seven years old, her baby sister squeezed under a fence and drowned in the neighbor's swimming pool. Although she never actually saw the corpse, she still has nightmares in which Dora's body, red and bloated, bobs beyond her reach like a candied apple. Sometimes, of late, her sister's cadaver flips over to reveal Calliope's face. So my wife's anger has a history. I accept that.

"I didn't mean to snap at you," Gillian says. "I'm just on edge."

She reaches over the car-seat, above our sleeping child, and squeezes my hand.

◇

We've already childproofed our apartment—forcing socket guards into the outlets, insulating extension cords with electrical tape—but, after the penny incident, Gillian grows determined to rid our home of all ingestible objects. She removes the magnets from the face of the refrigerator and unscrews the knobs from the doors to the stereo cabinet. My plants are banished to the highest shelves of my study, as is the fish tank, while the Tetramin flakes I feed to the gouramis must now be securely locked inside an iron bin along with Gillian's art supplies and my anti-seizure medication. After seven days of constant scrutiny and scouring, our apartment looks as though it has been picked clean by refugees. Then my wife discovers one of my old guitar picks inside the piano bench and she bursts into sobs.

"Why don't we hire a nanny?" I suggest. "We can afford it."

Afford is a subjective term. Maybe what I'm really saying is that hiring a nanny to look after Calliope seems cheaper than the psychological toll of not hiring one.

"I don't want to hire a nanny," insists Gillian. "That would just be another person to supervise...another person who might accidentally leave her coins out."

"You heard Dr. Frey, honey," I say. "It was a fluke. A one-off. Cal hasn't swallowed anything else in a week." I climb down to the living room carpet, where Calliope crawls in her pajamas while smacking together a pair of large plastic rings. "You're not going to swallow any more coins, darling, are you?"

"She's not going to have a chance to," says Gillian—but I've made my wife smile. I have the habit of negotiating with small children and domestic animals as though they're capable of understanding, even though rationally I realize that they're not. Gillian always finds this quirk highly amusing. Once she caught me urging our Siamese fighting fish not to overeat, and we laughed about it for months. That was during her pregnancy, but it already seems like a lifetime ago. Now she joins us on the floor and starts buttoning Calliope's sweater. "Let's get her ready for bed," she says. Seconds later, she lets out a profanity-laced cry of horror.

"What's wrong?" I ask

"Look!"

She draws Calliope towards us. Our daughter looks fearful, but otherwise unscathed. Nonetheless, I assess her closely—as though searching for a hidden image in a cluttered drawing. Nothing. I sense that this is Gillian's version of a Rorschach test, and that I am failing miserably.

"Look," pleads Gillian. "She's lost a button."

I still don't notice anything amiss, at first. None of the buttons appear misaligned and I discern no visible gaps. Yet, sure enough, an extra eyelet scars the lower hem of the girl's sweater. I hook my index finger through the knit to satisfy myself that the perforation is not an optical illusion. It isn't. Two torn loops of pink yarn mark the site of the missing wooden disk.

"What now?" asks Gillian.

"Now we get her ready for bed," I say. "Not a big deal. Honestly, it's probably lying in her playpen at my mother's."

"She swallowed it," answers Gillian. "I just know she did."

"Okay, so maybe she swallowed it," I concede. "It's not a razor blade. Swallowing a wooden button isn't the end of the world."

"This is much larger than one button," replies Gillian. She is already removing the offending sweater. "Good God, Dave. Please tell me you understand that."

"Of course, I understand that," I assure her, although I'm not exactly certain what I'm confessing to understand.

"Well, show it then," Gillian orders.

"Okay," I agree. "What do you want me to do?"

Gillian looks me over, her pale brow furrowed. Maybe she is searching my face for a hint of sarcasm or insincerity. If that's her goal, she'll find none. "Why don't you tell Cal a bedtime story while I cut off these buttons?" she finally suggests—sounding relieved. "This is my fault," she continues. "What kind of mother buys her baby a sweater with wooden buttons?" My wife insists on apologizing to me, and then to Calliope, although our daughter appears far more interested in my impassioned rendition of Goldilocks. Every time I say, "*and this one was just right*," I squeeze my daughter's nose, and she gurgles with glee. Soon she is sleeping, smiling dreamily. I cradle her tiny frame back and forth—awed that such an innocent creature can cause so much grief—while, in the background, I hear the blades of Gillian's scissors snipping through wool.

◊

I phone my teaching assistant early the next morning and ask him if he'd like to lecture on "Lycophytes and Ferns." He jumps at the opportunity. I've only been out of graduate school for five years myself, but teaching—as much as I do enjoy it—no longer gives me the rush that it did when my only opportunities occurred while filling in for my mentor. In the same way, our family's frequent visits to Dr. Frey's office have lost their novelty. Eleven months ago, a bout of diarrhea or a fever of 99.8 was enough to have me calling our pediatrician's answering service at four o'clock in the morning. Now, although Calliope carries a penny, and possibly a wooden button, inside her gut, I am not even remotely alarmed. I suppose that I've come to view our daughter's health as inexorable, a certainty of the cosmos.

Dr. Frey shares office space with three other pediatricians in a low-slung stucco building across the boulevard from the hospital. When one steps across the threshold of the outer vestibule, a motion-sensor triggers a recording of "Pop! Goes the Weasel." Inside the waiting room, assorted toys lay strewn over the padded floor-mats like rubble.

The doctor squeezes us in before her first scheduled patient. She is wearing a shapeless lab coat once again, her auburn hair tied back—but I have trouble forgetting the curves that I now know lurk beneath her drab, loose-fitting uniform. I let Gillian do the talking, while I ponder our pediatrician's romantic status. She does not wear a wedding ring. Deep down, of course, I have no intention of cheating on Gillian. Even if I could. I'm more like the loyal employee who enjoys testing out his boss's office chair, once in a while, when his employer is away, even kicking his feet up on the chief's desk, knowing full well that he's never actually going to run the show. I catch Calliope reaching for the coffee cup full of pens on the pediatrician's desk and I stick out my tongue to distract her.

"That *is* a big button," I hear Dr. Frey say. Gillian is holding her thumb and her index finger approximately one centimeter apart. "But luckily the walls of the digestive tract have some built-in accommodation, so I wouldn't worry too much about the size....You didn't happen to notice if she ever passed that penny."

"She hasn't," Gillian assures her. "And believe me, I've checked."

"Good. That's important," replies our pediatrician. "We want to make sure we have a running inventory of everything that's inside her."

My wife looks alarmed. "What do you mean? You're not saying we're going to keep letting her swallowing things."

"Not if we can help it," agrees Dr. Frey. "But no method of prevention is foolproof. Children have a way of getting what they want." As if on cue, Calliope reaches for the pen cup again. This time, the pediatrician sidetracks her by producing a large orange sponge-ball. "That doesn't mean letting your guard down. Don't get me wrong. That just means accepting that, even with your guard up, she's bound to outsmart you some of the time."

"So there's no medication? No therapy?"

"Not for pica. If it is pica, that is," says the pediatrician. "Of course, twelve months is a very early age of onset....In any case, the best thing we can do is hope that she outgrows it. Most patients do."

"And in the meantime?"

"Be vigilant. Put yourself in Calliope's shoes whenever you enter a new environment, always ask yourself what you would do if you were a twelve-month-old girl looking to ingest small objects."

"For how long?"

"Unfortunately, I can't give you a firm answer. I wish I could," says

Dr. Frey. "Some cases last months. Others last years....And in a small percentage of cases...." She waves her hand. "That's a long way off. "Let's not go there," she concludes. "The bottom line is that the overwhelming majority of children like Calliope ultimately go on to lead normal, happy lives, so there's no reason to think she won't."

I'm tempted to ask Dr. Frey what percentage of *all* people lead "happy lives"—whether happy lives aren't by definition *ab*normal—but I recognize that she'd find such questions transgressive. Instead, I lead my family back across the waiting room, where a conclave of other sickly children has already congregated, their mothers worshipping modern medicine to the timeless strains of "*Pop! Goes the Weasel.*"

◊

It's only ten o'clock when we return from the doctor's—too late to justify the commute to the university, yet still early enough for almost anything else. I urge Gillian to take advantage of my presence. Ever since Calliope entered our lives, my wife has had only two afternoons each week to devote to her compositions, while my mother plays babysitter, so she rarely has a stretch of uninterrupted work-time that lasts more than three or four hours. I'm optimistic that a full day as an artist will help her unwind. Secretly, I'm also thrilled to have my daughter all to myself. While Gillian fashions shredded milk cartons into a three-dimensional portrait of Picasso and Braque kissing, Calliope and I take turns pressing buttons on a machine that mimics animal sounds. Every time my daughter makes the donkey bray or the turkey gobble, a perverse part of me hopes that the widowed sisters upstairs will phone the animal warden. Mistaking a children's toy for a barnyard would certainly undermine their credibility with the landlord. Alas, after a few minutes, Calliope grows tired of synthetic *oinking* and *mooing*. What she'd much rather do is lick the machine's console with her tongue. As a compromise, I offer her a jar of Gerber's peach puree and a glass of cow's milk. That's about when our perfect afternoon of father-daughter bonding begins to unravel.

My wife pokes her head into the kitchen to ask if we've seen her grandmother's silver thimble. "It's always in my sewing basket," she insists. "I also can't find my jade earrings, and the zipper from one of my winter boots is gone."

If I hadn't known Gillian for thirteen years, I might take these concerns more seriously. But I'm aware that my wife hasn't worn her jade earrings anytime in recent memory, probably since I escorted her to her Barnard College formal, and I didn't even know that she owned a sewing basket. The reality is that, instead of working on her collage, she has spent the morning combing our apartment for missing odds and ends. "Don't you think we should take her in for another X-ray?" presses Gillian. "Just to be safe?" I am about to tell her that there is absolutely nothing to worry about, that our daughter may be the healthiest one-year-old in Brooklyn—the Jack LaLanne of toddlerdom—when Calliope vomits up the baby food. Then she starts sobbing and hugs her arms to her tummy. Within seconds, with a vigor that would cheer the most partisan advocates of female domesticity, my wife assumes the role of nursemaid and I am banished from the room.

I try to look in on my two women every few hours, but each time Gillian waves me away. I hear her drawing a bath for Calliope, helping the girl into a fresh set of dry clothes. The last rays of the twilight are already losing their grasp on the fire escape when my wife finally tiptoes into my study. Her face is ashen.

"How is she?" I ask.

"Sick. Her stomach aches. She needs an X-ray," replies Gillian. "This is a catastrophe waiting to happen, Dave. I'm not sure why you can't see that."

My wife sits on the arm on the leather sofa, toying nervously with her wedding band. I know she is waiting for me to validate her concerns—to concede that we are in the midst of a crisis—but I am hurting too. To paraphrase the late Dr. April, the time has finally come to salute the matrimonial magpie.

"I've had enough of this endless game of good parent, bad parent," I say, making an effort to keep my voice soft and steady. "I love Cal just as much as you do."

"I know you do…." Gillian interjects.

"Let me finish," I continue. "I love Cal. And I love you too. But that doesn't mean I have to stand idly by while you act like a madwoman. X-rays aren't benign. You do realize that, don't you? You keep worrying about copper leaching from pennies, but X-raying a baby is just a step below sticking her inside the microwave." I'm going to add that a trip to the emergency room exposes children to all sorts of pathogens, raises the risk of whooping cough and viral meningitis and God knows what else, but now Gillian is weeping softly, so I cut myself short.

"I can't help myself, sometimes," she says. "I know what Cal feels like. Some days I just want to run out into the street and start stuffing strange objects down my throat until I can't breathe anymore. Doesn't that sound insane?"

"Not at all," I soothe her. "It just sounds like you're under a lot of stress."

"But I've *always* felt this way," says Gillian. "Not about the strange objects, but about letting go. I never told you this, but once last year, while you were away doing field work, I was seized with an overwhelming impulse to run into the street and throw myself at the first man I could find." Her face is buried in her hands, her voice barely audible. "I wouldn't really do that, of course. But somehow the idea of it made everything seem so easy....You must hate me, don't you?"

My wife is trembling, and I wrap my arms around her. That night, we make love for the first time in months.

◊

Breakfast finds Calliope's retching a distant memory. Our daughter sits in her highchair, banging her spoon gleefully against the attached plastic tray. Gillian is also in good spirits. Without any prompting, she suggests hiring a sitter for the evening and going to the movies. I am jubilant. Relieved. I coast through the workday high on tranquility, raising past test scores for any student who asks and assembling a bouquet of exotic irises from the university's hothouse for my secretary. That night, we watch Humphrey Bogart in *The Caine Mutiny* at the Atlantic Avenue Playhouse, then share a carafe of red wine over pasta at our favorite bistro on Steinhoff Street. Gillian's interrogation of our sitter, an auburn-haired actress named Lauren, remains well within the bounds of normal parenting. The following morning, despite some reluctance, she even agrees to leave Calliope with my mother and stepdad. "But your mom has to promise to keep the ringer on at all times," Gillian demands. "None of their napping bullshit." So I kiss my glowing wife at the door, where she has already donned a paint-splattered smock, drop off my hale, peony-cheeked daughter with her grateful grandmother, and slide into my role as benevolent junior professor and mild-mannered botanist with unprecedented jaunt and alacrity. I catch my reflection in the subway doors—a bookish creature in well-worn tweeds, his briefcase on his lap—and I am content enough with what I see.

My reprieve proves short-lived. I have some advance warning, because Gillian has phoned my mother, looking for me, at fifteen minute intervals since four o'clock. When I arrive at our apartment, carrying Calliope on my shoulders, the living room looks like it has been ravaged by a cyclone. All of the furniture stands gathered at the center of the carpet, as though in preparation for painting the walls—or, the ominous idea visits me, in preparation for a massive bonfire. Gone is any effort to keep ingestible objects above waist-level. A open toolbox, its screws and washers gleaming, rests menacingly beneath the halogen lamp. Gillian sits in a bare corner of the floor, where the piano once stood, leaning against the exposed plaster. Blood drips from a gash on her left temple.

"I can't find them," she says. "I swear I've looked everywhere."

I don't doubt her. "What can't you find?" I ask.

"You'll forgive me, won't you?" pleads Gillian. "We'll get her an X-ray, and she'll be okay, and then you'll forgive me...."

"Of course, I'll forgive you. Now what happened?"

My wife explains that some of the safety pins she has been using on her Picasso-Braque collage are missing. "I've only used eighty-four on the canvas, but the box is completely empty. That's a difference of sixteen safety pins!"

Calliope starts patting on the top of my head, then slapping my scalp with her palms. I stabilize her leg with one hand and hold my glasses straight with the other.

"Try to think clearly," I say. "You don't really believe she's swallowed sixteen safety pins?"

"I don't know what to believe," replies Gillian. "The safety pins are missing. They had to go somewhere, didn't they?"

"But we've been watching her? Don't you think we'd have noticed if she swallowed a box of pins?"

"Who knows? Maybe Lauren let her guard down last night," says Gillian. "Or maybe Cal has been sneaking out of her crib."

"So what now?" I ask. "We can't take the girl in for an X-ray every time we're short a paperclip or a feather."

Gillian says nothing. She remains slumped in the corner, her knees drawn to her chest beneath the smock. Streaks of eyeliner coat her cheeks and a strand of dried blood connects her forehead to the corner of her mouth. I carry Calliope into the kitchen and return to the living room with a damp paper towel. Silently, she takes the towel and salves her wound.

"How deep is that cut?" I ask. "Maybe you should get it checked out."

Gillian shrugs. "That's the least of my concerns," she says. She reaches for my hand and claps her fingers around my wrist. I can feel the desperation in her grip. "One X-ray, okay? For my peace of mind." My wife's eyes are wide and hopeful. "Just once, Dave. I promise. After that we'll figure something else out."

I survey the chaos of our apartment, the collage of bureaus and chairs and household artifacts piled high like a monument to Conestoga wagons. Upstairs, the widowed sisters are playing big band music on their stereo, filling the entire building with the rhythms of Glenn Miller and Tommy Dorsey.

I nod. "One X-ray," I agree. "For peace of mind."

My concession triggers an unexpected burst of tears from Calliope. I set her down on the parquet and she crawls into her mother's lap. The sobs ebb quickly, replaced by a look of wonder and a gush of babbling. Then, after a clap of silence, our daughter utters her first full word: "*EAT!*" It is unmistakable. She repeats her only word over and over again during dinner, a mantra of abstract resolve, seemingly immune to all of the cow's milk and pureed fruit that we can muster.

◊

Gillian is adamant that the X-ray cannot wait until morning. They're *pins*, she contends—they could perforate Calliope's intestines. Somehow, the *safety* aspect of the "safety pins" has slipped her mind, but I don't belabor the issue. I'd rather visit the pediatric emergency room on a weekday evening, when the traffic is relatively light, than on a school morning, when every aspiring, underage truant will be flailing in the throes of hypochondria. I'm also concerned about Gillian's forehead, which it turns out she has injured against the dishwasher door., When we reach the hospital, I urge her to have her wound checked out while I wait with our daughter—but she refuses. "I want to see the X-ray with my own eyes," she insists. "It's for your own good, Dave. It will keep you from having to hide anything from me."

"I wouldn't do that," I say—but we both know that I'm lying.

We inform the triage nurse that Calliope has swallowed a collection of safety pins, and she shepherds us into a semi-private alcove. A hospital gown and a cloth blanket lie neatly folded at the foot of a narrow bed. Two other beds share this recess, but at ten o'clock on a Tuesday night, they stand empty. On the wall nearby, a glossy poster warns against the early signs of dehydration. All around us, assorted monitors bleat their need for immediate attention.

Anticipating another lengthy wait, I've brought along the galleys for my article on morning glories and moonflowers to proofread. I spread my taxonomic charts out atop one of the empty beds. Meanwhile, Gillian braids Calliope's hair. Miraculously, the pediatric resident appears to serve us only moments later. It is Maia Clampitt once again. The would-be psychiatrist still has papers sticking out of her pockets, also a laminated card labeled: *Cheat Sheet for Pediatrics*. She looks as bewildered as ever.

"I'm actually not assigned to this bed, but I recognized your name on the chart, so I traded patients with Dr. Cobb," she tells us. "I've been reading up on pica all week. It's a fascinating illness—from a physician's perspective, that is." The young doctor removes a ballpoint pen from her coat. It contains no ink. She discards the pen, produces a second pen from a different pocket, and asks, "So what brings you in today?"

"She swallowed safety pins," explains Gillian. "Sixteen of them."

Dr. Clampitt frowns. "Six*teen*? I could have sworn it said six on her chart."

"If you already know what happened," snaps my wife, "why are you asking?"

I feel genuinely sorry for the beleaguered intern. Dr. Clampitt's face suffuses a deep pink, and she appears poised to say something, but then she thinks the better of it and sets about examining Calliope. She speaks to my daughter as though the girl is an adult—asking permission to listen to her lungs, warning her before she palpates her belly—and that makes me like the young shrink all the more. I can't help feeling that Dr. Clampitt and I are on the same team—that we share the solidarity of knowing that my daughter is fine, that it's Gillian we're actually treating with this workup.

"Everything sounds good," the intern declares, tucking her stethoscope back into her overflowing pocket. "I'm not too worried."

"But you'll order an X-ray?" pushes Gillian.

"Honestly, I think it's overkill," replies Dr. Clampitt. "She had one last week. But if it will make you sleep better...."

"It will," says Gillian.

"Thank you, doctor," I add. "We really do appreciate it."

So once again, my wife accompanies our daughter into the radiology suite while I purchase coffee from a vending machine. I scan the benches opposite the swinging doors, hoping to see Dr. Frey once more, but the only occupant this evening is a bearded maintenance worker napping away his break. I glance at my watch. It is already after midnight. My teaching assistant may gain yet another chance at the big stage. I'm debating whether I should call him now, or wait until the morning, when my family returns. While Calliope was being imaged, someone had bandaged my wife's forehead. Gauze now surrounds her skull like a headband.

"I know what you're thinking, Dave," says Gillian. "You're thinking that this is a colossal waste of time and that you could be home sleeping right now."

"That's not what I was thinking at all."

"Then what *were* you thinking?" asks Gillian.

"I was thinking that I want to make sure my daughter isn't going to die from a pin puncture," I reply. "And *then* I want to be home sleeping."

That seems to be the correct answer—or at least an acceptable one. Gillian smiles and caresses my cheek with her palm. I cup my hand over hers, squeezing gently. Then we return to our secluded alcove to wait.

On our prior visit to the ER, it required only twenty minutes to read my daughter's X-ray, so nothing prepares us for an hour-long delay. When Dr. Clampitt finally arrives, I'm expecting her to announce Calliope's clean bill of health. Instead, she says that Dr. Budge, the attending pediatrician, wishes to speak with us. "I'm sure it's nothing," I promise Gillian. "They probably lost the X-ray." But when Dr. Budge finally appears, sporting a bowtie beneath his hard grimace and hangdog jowls, he does not strike me as a man who would tolerate the loss of an X-ray. Maia Clampitt trails him at several paces, looking as though she fears a firing squad.

"I want to show you something," says Dr. Budge.

The pediatrician steps to a nearby workstation and we follow. He clicks several buttons on the computer monitor and types in Calliope's name. Without warning, her X-ray blankets the entire screen.

"Do you see that?" the doctor asks—tapping the image with a bare tongue depressor. "And that? And that? And that?"

I don't need to be a radiologist to recognize that something is amiss. The distinct outline of several safety pins is visible inside my daughter's stomach, as well as numerous white slivers that I soon realize are other pins captured at lateral angles. But that is not the worst that the image has to reveal. Where last week there had been one small coin, now there are at least six of various sizes. Dimes? Quarters? Foreign currency? Also two opaque squares that look like dice, a bent paperclip, and what resembles a trio of children's jacks. And then there are several other small white silhouettes of unidentifiable household detritus:

Thumbtacks? Marbles? Maybe the outline of an oblate wooden button? "Your daughter has been a busy young lady," declares Dr. Budge.

"So what do we do?" asks Gillian.

"Nothing," replies Dr. Budge. "We could put an endoscope down there, but the risk of perforation probably outweighs any benefit. Nobody every died from walking around with a few pins in her stomach. But you've got to keep a much better eye on this young lady—or she will end up swallowing something dangerous."

"We've been trying," pleads Gillian.

"Well, try harder," answers Dr. Budge. "Strap her down if you have to. Pica is serious business. When I was in the navy, Mrs. Hertz, a midshipman brought in a three-year-old who had swallowed an incendiary bullet." He presses another button on the keyboard and Calliope's innards vanish from the computer screen. "There's only one treatment for pica, I'm afraid. Growing an extra eye in the backs of your heads."

That's all the wisdom that the attending physician has to offer. "Follow up with your regular pediatrician," he says. "Come back if she develops any symptoms."

◊

We return home to an apartment that is bare and grim. With all of the furniture heaped in the centers of the rooms, the place conveys the impression that it will soon be vacated. I plug in the table lamps, but the incandescent bulbs cast shadows that make the naked walls appear even starker.

Calliope has fallen asleep in the cab, but now she is awake once again. Gillian announces that she'll put out daughter to bed. *On her own.* So I begin returning the living room furniture to its proper place, trying to remember the location of various bookshelves and bureaus, until the entire endeavor no longer seems worth the effort. Instead, I retreat into the bedroom to wait for Gillian. I cannot imagine how my wife managed to lug the king-size bed away from the wall, but I don't bother to move it back. I lack the energy. Lying on the unmoored bed feels a bit like testing out a new mattress in a showroom. In the next room, my wife's high-pitched voice croons "Bye, Bye Bunting." I doze off in my clothes.

When I wake up, several hours later, Gillian has still not come to bed.

I peek into Calliope's room. Our daughter rests on her back, a slash of light from the airshaft illuminating her neck and shoulders. She looks angelic. A warm evening breeze brows through the open window, billowing the drapes.

I find Gillian in the kitchen, seated at the dining table. A tall glass of milk stands in front of her, also a milk carton and a small mound of pennies. My wife glances in my direction as I enter, but says nothing. I'm still reflecting on what *I* want to say when she places one of the pennies on her tongue and draws it into her mouth. Then she sips from the glass of milk and swallows.

I sit down opposite her and reach for her hand. She pulls it away.

"I'm putting myself in her shoes," my wife says. "That's what we should have been doing all along. *Both* of us."

Gillian takes two more pennies from the pile and swallows one, gagging violently as the coin goes down. She places the other coin in the palm of my hand. It is a 1992 penny, minted in Denver. It weighs hardly an ounce, yet it feels heavier than a sack of lead against my skin.

Together, we watch the copper coin as it rests on my bare flesh, and I understand that we are both waiting for me to swallow it. That is what love is about, isn't it? Swallowing the ingestible. I am sure I will do it too—and yet I don't move. I can feel the muscles of my gullet constricting, my tonsils engorging with blood. I want to be the man who will swallows a roll of pennies for the woman he loves, but that man is no longer me. The throat of my life has already narrowed too far.

The Women

Jane Hilberry

They're both Midwestern, awed by the gold
of California sun. He never suspects

they meet, compare his gifts—none, thank god, alike—
praise the way he comports himself, always

the gentleman, taking the street side when they walk.
The older one's a better cook, better gardener. It's right

that she should live with him. They work this out
at the glass table, bare feet burrowed in the fur

of his beloved dog. My God! one thinks, I see
how he fell in love with her. The poppies nod.

The glasses of iced tea begin to sweat.

Baiting

Jenny Hanning

When the good don't die young they grow slowly old wishing that they had.
They become the dog-kickers.

    The steady loss of glory is a soul dividing state.
You know what I mean—when you see a photograph and the jaw line is so
sharp, the man so unforgivably lovely, and look now. Now, look—just look.

    What's that? What *is* that?
Well, what's anyone who was pretty and ceases to be so. There's no question
mark, because we are speaking rhetorically.

    Get with it.

        Follow along.
Elvis, say—

    was he still stacking the girls like French toast? When they touched
his sagging cheek did their fingertips come away orange?

    Isn't vanity a sin?

        But isn't it the most forgivable?
Like the prophets who mislaid the future, but did it so the hero would win.
They baited him like a dog. Jabbed him with certain failure until his
sweetness buckled under rage and then sent him,

    frothing and merciless,

      out to redeem his own self and his own name and his own
    pride and afterward there were
no enemies left,

    or children of the enemy,

       or the enemies' dogs,

          or their thatch roofed barns. There was nothing left,
afterward. So if I told you that I wanted to be one of those children raised
in India by wolves, or brew beer and keep bees for Set—

    because *isn't* life chaos?

      and because *who doesn't* enjoy a walk in the rain?—

             who could blame me?

If I told you that I believed a snake swallowed the moon then made love
to her while the sun's back was turned and that hot wax spilled onto my chest
             makes me think of flight, would you deny it?
                    How could you? Or anyone?
So if he demands you know his name it's only because so many others have
refused him. Ozymandias, and all that jazz. Ask a child what an avatar is and
they'll show you a cartoon-self,
             a video game,
                    an upright-walking tiger, cannons on his back.
   We've long lost track of God on earth,
             the crocodile that eats your child, the sparrow that couriers souls.

Paradise Farms

Karina Borowicz

To the hiss of cicadas I kept picking hand over fist
dropping the big black berries into the white pail
they give you when you wander in trying to look calm
not desperate after driving out there like a maniac
craving not so much berries as the act of gathering from the branch
plucking gently from the stem rolling one after another
into the palm till you can't hold any more, then the heavy
kerplunk in the bucket, that simple three-part gesture repeated
till aching, with which I so needed to stain my hands

The Dog, the Garden, and the Ornament

James O'Brien

The brown dog walked into my lawn. I almost did not recognize the dog as a dog in the dying light. I was kneeling and planting marigolds. I had been digging holes with my favorite trowel since the afternoon. Guests were coming over the next day for brunch. I wanted the garden to look good. Marigolds look good and they look better when they are well planted and set straight. So I had been planting good marigolds in good holes with my good trowel and I was sure it would all look very good.

But then the dog came.

It trotted right in. It came through the butterfly bush at the end of my lawn. I would not have minded so much if it had come through my compost heap at the other side. The dog looked at me and urinated on my marigolds. It must have been female because it squatted. I yelled at the dog. It continued urinating. I worried about its urine being acidic and ruining the soil's pH. I threw a chunk of clay at the dog and told it to go. It stopped urinating. The dog inched up to me and stared me in the eyes. Its nose leveled with my nose. Small infected pustules shone where its whiskers should have been. Scars ran along its muzzle in depressed rakes. The dog growled.

I told it to get off my lawn. The dog did not move. The dog growled again. It snapped its teeth and barred them. Its canines were white at the tip and yellow at the root. Its breath smelled like meat left out too long. It pulled its ears back. One ear was torn and winched back crooked against the dog's head. I bumped its nose with the flat of my good trowel. The dog stepped back. It turned its head to the side as if confused. The dog lunged at me. I fell back. The dog rushed for my neck. I stabbed the brown dog with my gardening trowel. The brown dog yelped then whined then kept on yelping. The trowel stuck from between the dog's wide shoulder blades. The handle wobbled as the dog ran. The trowel was buried two inches into its hide. I stood back. My feet felt small in my gardening clogs. The dog tossed around the flower bed. It tore my petunias and rolled my marigolds flat as stone. It bled on their petals and their leaves. It ground them into the sod. They looked like small butterflies about to take off. They did not.

The trowel slipped from the dog's wound. Its head glimmered red. It sat there glimmering red next to my red petunias. The dog whimpered a little and snapped at something I could not see. It salivated and shook. I felt a little bad. I picked up the trowel and walked up to the dog and dug the trowel into its throat. Then the dog stopped whimpering.

I hauled the dog by its legs and dropped it in the compost pile and buried it under some rotting shrubbery. I buried the dog well but its legs stood straight up through the compost. I could even see it in the new dark. They looked like a quadrant of stunted bean-runners without any beans. I tried to push its legs down under the compost but I could not. Rigor mortis must have set in. That would not do. I wanted my lawn to look pleasing to my guests and four strange bean runners would not look pleasant to normal people. I tried to think of what to do. If my guests saw the weird bean runners they would think I was weird too. I wanted to be normal. To be as good as my garden.

◇

I carried the dead dog to my trash can. I shoved it down head first but the dog would not fit. I thought about chopping its legs off with my hacksaw. But then I worried about the hacksaw getting dull. I needed the hacksaw to trim some branches the next weekend and a dull hacksaw is no good for trimming. I carried the dog back to my garden. I set it next to the marigolds. I left it there next to me and began replanting my flowers. I smoothed each petal and each leaf until they were straight and perfect. I stood them in their plots and tamped the soil to hold them there. They looked fine. But there was still a wide barren run where the dog had tossed around. I had nothing to fill the barren run with and it was too late to go to the gardening store.

The dead dog kept staring at me in the same way it had stared at me when it had walked into my lawn. I got a little angry at it again for all this trouble. I kicked its stomach and the dog fell over like a toppled flower pot. I set it back up and stroked its head. The dog was not so bad like this. It did not urinate. It did not growl. It did not tramp around my garden. The dog was frozen in a concentrated expression. It looked quite dedicated. I set it between my marigolds and petunias like a lawn ornament.

When my guests came over the next day we ate cantaloupe and omelets and sipped mimosas. We sat on my porch and looked out at my garden. My guests all asked me how I kept my garden so well. The lawn ornament fascinated them. They studied it for a long time. One of my guests asked where I had purchased it. I told her I had made it. She looked impressed. Then she left. Another said that it completed my lawn. Then he left. They all left very suddenly after each observed my garden and my curious lawn ornament there. Maybe they were in awe of the dedication I had put into making the garden so very perfect. I figure my guests probably went out to all the gardening stores in the area looking for something similar to my lawn ornament. But the whole thing is you cannot buy a good lawn. It takes dedication. Just a little dedication.

Garlic

Dawn Tefft

A pert resistance to the ascendancy of sugar.
It speaks without cloying
or fussing or looking for the bodies of angels.
More like pictures of heavens spinning with gas,
planets slowly exploding
in skins made of the smallest-fitting electrons.

The earth in its flesh like a root.
A perfume that refuses to be washed off of lips
like nights stolen from God, upending
relationships with wives. No other kiss
like this one—it means to be noticed.

A pubescent light rustling its name in the dark.

Demanding in the voice of all that is centrifugal
and earth-born to be released from its globe.

Sharp-toothed tongue, sword of
La Mancha, undulating in a rock quarry of stars,
unimaginable vein of ore.
A skin that can't contain its own nature.
Small warrior.
Falls easily in love.

Birth

Noah Gershman

For as long as I knew her
my mother insisted
she'd won me in a poker game
one summer in the south of France.
The story made everybody laugh,
but when she died I found a photo.
In a sunlit parlor, wall of windows
overlooking the sea, at a table
are a dozen glamorous women,
knockouts in hairdos and headscarves
and beads, smoking long cigarettes
and playing what appears to be
seven card stud. Some are smiling,
others are serious, my mother
looks focused and terribly concerned.
The jackpot is enormous with babies.
Most of them are crying, but I,
two or three years old at least, am calm
and waiting, in my navy blazer
and seersucker shorts.

Sidewalking

KC Eib

Surely my apprehensions will sink with the setting sun. Strewn topsy-turvy across the threadbare carpet—black electrical tape, Marlboro Lights, powder, maroon lipliner, Wintergreen Certs, ibuprofen, a single condom—my personal belongings are stashed quickly inside my mini-satchel where a folded wad of bills and state ID have already been secured. The leather satchel, swollen with more minutiae than I need, slings over my shoulder. I grab a disposable camera off my steamer trunk, snap a self-portrait in the doorway to my adobe studio, and step into the nearly night.

Snapshot: Late Summer, Albuquerque, 1997. My mother and I stand with plastic grocery bags in both hands. She and her boyfriend drove the two-day trip to settle me into my new apartment. We wear the same shorts and t-shirts from two days prior when the van broke down in Small Town, Kansas. Our eyes squint against the setting sun; smiles appear grimaced with our longing for respite. A thorny bush grows next to the doorway. It will reach the rooftop soon, if it is not trimmed.

The day's last light dips steadily behind the Sandia Mountains. I stride along the paved frames of sidewalk, breathe in the heat steaming in waves off the pavement. It's my first time to perform in New Mexico, and I hold doubts about my decision to walk, worry about how my appearance might be received. The warmth in the southwest wind, rustling through my sculpted hair and skirt, reminds me that things are different this time. I feel confident, playful in my cork platforms and celluloid bouffant. This is not the Windy City where a lakefront gust might rip my wig clean off my head. This is not the hardened streets of Chicago where catcalls hiss and whistles teem with broken bottles shattered along the brick buildings behind me. Welcome to Albuquerque where attitudes are more laid-back; my new home eases me into her landscape with a mild breath of late summer breeze.

I veer onto Yale Boulevard where a cyclist hollers from the bike lane, "You go, girl!" Uh-huh, watch me. All my cutting and taping and shaping and painting and fashioning my last-minute makeover; all my production anxieties questioning whether the costume would really come together, dissipate with the biker's shout-out. My gait sways further into the swing of my hips and sasses in my high-step. I shimmy my wig back and forth, throw my head back, and direct my eyes toward the blushing horizon.

So what if the wig didn't come together the way I planned it. What else could I have done? Despite the overabundance of possessions I hauled to New Mexico, nowhere amidst my milk crates of license plates, Great Aunt Edna's defunct Frigidaire, the cardboard boxes of phone receivers, medical tubing, foam and plastic curlers, or rolls of bubble wrap, could I find my manila folder of film negatives—for whatever reason, they hadn't survived the move. In my frantic search, I dumped boxfuls of feathers and goggles and wine corks and cassette tapes and bangles in haphazard piles. Any semblance of order to my pack rat realm crumbled under the surging adrenaline of hope coupled with urgency.

More than anything, I needed the negatives. Those deep auburn strips that complemented my light complexion. The UNM photography department donated a few strips of rejects from students, but I could not accept a shoulder-length wig for this performance. I wanted to be bigger and better than my original Chicago performance; the walk to the club promised high visibility, and I wanted nothing less than awe from my onlookers. The walk measured a good mile down Central Avenue, which made the total trip nearly two miles, including my hike along Yale. If I was going to turn heads, I wanted to do it in big hair. In the end, I supplemented with rolls of undeveloped film bought in family-size multi-packs from Smith's grocery store.

The choice to walk in full drag seemed obvious at first. Without a car, or at least an extra set of hands, the costume proved too bulky for lugging along in sections. When I first moved to Albuquerque, not a full month earlier, I bought a little red wagon for hauling props and costumes around on these sorts of escapades. My investment made sense at the time, but I didn't know logistically where I'd park the wagon or how I might watch my belongings once I arrived at the club. Checking a little red wagon like a coat seemed a bit impractical, perhaps ridiculous.

Not that I knew for certain the club even had a coat check. I just didn't know enough about the Albuquerque scene to trust my judgments.

Drag queens in Chicago had always spooked me a little. I used to carry a tackle box of makeup around with me until Anita said, "Girl, don't be leaving your shit out for everybody to be in your business. These bitches play dirty. You'll end up with crushed glass in your powder. Ain't no Miss America ever had pockmarks." Typical Anita, I thought, full of her nightly dramas. But later at the Halsted Street Fair, Daisy Mae told me Vortex quit doing shows. She put it to me something like, "Ain't no freak-and-nigger-in-free nights, so take your happy ass to some other home." Some street queen threw acid on another performer's face. To burn, to scar: why did it always have to be the face? I must have been naïve or lucky or both in my Chicago days. The worst that happened to me was the night I performed with Pussy Tourette at a drag race and got my purse stolen. I still think Pussy did it. Dirty bitch. Took six months to replace my ID. I hoped Albuquerque wasn't the wicked step-sister of Chicago, but I was decided: What couldn't be worn wouldn't be taken.

No sooner do I turn off Yale and onto Central when a sun-bleached blue van pulls alongside the curb. The van's side door slides open, revealing a woman with greasy, stringy hair and blowfish eyes. If her eyes weren't stuck in a state of perpetual surprise, I'd covet their wideness. She flops out of the rusty van, her legs spindly and full of bounce.

"Where's the fashion show?" she asks, eyes bulging. I pretend she's reveling in my getup.

The idea of a fashion show sounds like good times, but I must confess to her, "I haven't heard of any fashion shows."

"Oh..." Her hand waves up and down in correspondence to the flicker of her eyes along my outfit. "I just thought..."

"No," I inform her, knowing that drag and fashion do not necessarily hold synonymous connotations, "I'll be performing at Pulse in their drag show." Her face sours in a shriveled scrunch. Confirmation: Mere drag does not elevate me to a heightened state of glamour. As if all drag must be tragically unfashionable by nature: gaudy, outdated, and unflattering to a male body squeezed and cinched and taped into protesting bulges. Where does all that manhood go, anyway? "Tucked," we say, as though it were an innocuous act, like putting a babe to bed.

Tucking. Well, it involves shoving the balls back inside a forgotten abdominal cavity, a mysterious and lost cavern, where the testicles formed in gestation. Once the balls drop down into the scrotum after birth, the cavity remains. What else could nature have had in mind with all that extra storage? Then there's the penis itself. Both the scrotum and penis are pulled back along the taint and duct-taped to butt cheeks. Okay, maybe this wasn't what nature had in mind. Those butt cheeks better be shaved if the tape is going to come off in one quick easy pull. Yes, I said easy, as in *tres facile*—like the Simplicity sewing patterns said in fine print on their envelopes when I was growing up. Those patterns were never easy, let alone *very easy*. In elementary school, Mom attempted to sew our family's Halloween costumes every year. One year, Dad wore devil horns Mom had sewn; they looked more like swollen, limp penises drooping off his head. Ah, the sacrifices we make for fashion. Maybe it's the fact that someone has said it's easy that makes us bound and determined to make that shit work. I'm convinced being truly fashionable means not being able to take a piss when you want; that is, if you can manage to take a piss at all.

Here I stand on the corner of Yale and Central, the greater portion of my body bound with duct tape: the wig to my head, the skirt around my waist, and my dick to my ass. I won't be peeing any time soon and need to be on my way.

The woman asks for the time and place of the show, a nice gesture, though the speculative look on her face remains an *Oh no, Hell no*! In any case, the conversation cuts short: drag does not equal fashion. Before she hefts herself into the van, I persuade her to have a picture taken with me in front of the No Parking sign. She obliges me with an extra solo shot clicked in front of The Frontier Mexican Restaurant before the van's sliding door swallows her up—limp, stringy hair and all.

Snapshot: Chicago, 1994. I am dressed in red bikini underwear with blue pinstripes. My body is shaved in its entirety. You can see my bones jutting out: ribs, collarbones, pointy elbows and knees. What you can't see is my dick, which has been tucked away. I point with both hands to where it should be. "Look, Ma, no dick!" My face is already painted and floats in a warm glow above my body. I am standing in front of a window overlooking a side street in Chicago. My kingdom awaits me below.

When I first put the costume together in Chicago, I had no wig. Well, I had one, but I puked in it. It was a late night after a show at Vortex with no one to hold my hair back in the john while I hurled the syrupy mistake of *another Black Sambuca, please.* It shouldn't have taken much to wash the wig out, but I wasn't ready to dredge up the details of Sambuca's man. He picked me up in the men's room, in a bathroom stall to be precise. I staggered out of the stall, asking with all my girlish charm, "Are there chunks in my hair?" He told me he'd walk me home, but we ended up going back to his place for a nightcap. Then he dumped me in the streets with my wig in clumps and the sun peeking over the horizon. The remainder of the journey I trudged alone, hoping to reach home before anyone I knew from my light-of-day life recognized me. Talk about draggedy-ass; my afterbar appearance was a tragic statement in taste. Without question, no fashion about it.

I don't know why I didn't wash the wig out and get on with it. I looked at wigs like underwear: one runny fart and they were done. When things go to shit, buy new, right? Of course, I wouldn't keep a soiled pair of shorts lying around the apartment for a month while I thought about it. But keep in mind a good wig isn't cheap. I'd never washed a wig; its luster and style would be lost. Others would know immediately the wig was a wig, but what did I care. I was broke and my alter ego Miss Evie wanted out.

There's something about being in a room full of smoke and dim lights and whatever kind of self-imposed, altered state of consciousness you can imagine that makes all sorts of things go unnoticed in a bar: split ends, lines of coke shared on a bar table, a plastered queen tripping down a flight of stairs with her pantyhose around her ankles. Maybe it's not that these things go unnoticed but that they are unremarkable. Anything that goes unacknowledged may as well not exist in the first place.

But I can't pretend not to notice when it's my own life I see, though there are days when I think it would be easier. Once I'm aware of something, I can't seem to let it go: I get caught up in what I think others might say about me. No way in hell was I about to knowingly go out to a club with dried vomit in my hair. However, I didn't have the money for a new wig. This was not the time for sulking over Sambuca's Man or avoiding the need for a wig. Berlin's monthly Drag Race approached; several shows had passed since I appeared onstage as Miss Evie and the regulars from the club kept urging me for more. I had no idea how to top my previous acts: a scissored-tribute to Lorraina Bobbitt followed up with a messy Jimi Hendrix number involving saran wrap, fruit, and the American flag from my father's casket. But I couldn't think of letting another show slip away without an appearance. I had to find a wig and fast.

Necessity must breed inspiration. I'd recently received a promotion to a customer service position at the F & M Drugstore where I cashiered as my day job. The managers assigned me all sorts of special tasks no one else wanted to do, like organizing toothbrushes by brand and style or stocking the magazine racks, which meant coming up with my own system of organization. While checking the pick-up dates of unclaimed film, my creative impulse awoke. No one had kept up with the task and it seemed a waste to scrap so much film. There were enough negatives to construct a full shoulder-length wig built around a film-canister base. The whole thing could be secured to my head with electrical tape.

The final product emerged as a waterfall of filmstrips falling around my face with the occasional coil or twist of film adding a lifelike undulation to the body of the wig. The black electrical tape proved to be the proper tool for binding its shape in a sound and supple form. Tape has always been a better friend to me than hairspray. None of the hair maintenance I loathed, all the transformative allure I longed for.

Snapshot: Summer, 1987. My hair is first wet then sprayed into tiny curls atop my head. I look like I have Jheri curls. This effect requires a full hour of work for Jules to accomplish. My receding hairline already shows at age sixteen. This moment will be one of the few times I remember having curls or wave to my hair. Later, when I am alone, I try accomplishing the same effect with toothpaste. I smell minty fresh, but fail to produce any curls.

With the blue van merging into a stream of vehicles along Central, my stride lengthens, back arches; I continue my course along a newly imagined runway. I don't need a catwalk to become Miss Fashion Show Extraordinaire. The throng of eyes from car windows and storefronts energizes my supermodel outlook. Thrills wave through me.

A large group of customers congregates outside The Double Rainbow, where the cool kids sip iced mochas in study groups. The café looks more like a human aquarium with scenesters floating in schools of overcrowded thought. Tables line the edge of the sidewalk; elbowroom remains a premium on the outskirts of the shop. A bubble of chatty women spills onto the sidewalk, forcing me to break my stride in order to weave through the crowd. I pause in front of the shop's entryway, swivel to my right and draw my disposable camera to my eyes with a keen sense of awareness. I frame my face by raising elbows up and out.

Snapshot: Childhood. We are the perfect family: Father, mother, two daughters and son arranged by age and height. I am the one at the bottom right with dirty blonde hair combed across my forehead. Mom has dressed the five of us in matching red vests, as if we are a traveling show. Our smiles are identical, every one of us. The composition is overly contemplated, too perfectly arranged to believe those manufactured smiles say anything you can trust about our home life.

The patrons waiting at the counter pose with peace signs, exaggerated smiles, and tongues protruding at my gaze. A girlish giggle escapes me. The crowd becomes enamored with the idea of being photographed. I nearly forget about myself with the vibe emanating from the posers on the other side of my lens; but two women, both with dreads and reeking of patchouli, ask if they can have their photo taken with me. It evolves into an all-out photo shoot. Complete strangers huddle together for the shot and just as quickly as we have come together for the ephemeral click of the shutter we drift back to our own agendas: tables drip with loose-leaf papers, the long line trails toward the door and more sundown-sidewalk calls me to carry on.

The two women; whose patchouli is not enough to mask the sweat and pot skulking somewhere beneath their outer layers, tag along for my walk. They tell me they're passing through with the Rainbow Family and out looking to have a good time. I wait for the communal joint or pills, neither of which reside in my purse, but they ramble on about some boy they chased through California who mistakenly landed them in Albuquerque instead of Denver. We're not more than a few blocks into their story when a motorcycle cop rumbles to a halt at the curbside.

"What's going on?" he asks as he pulls himself from his machine and lumbers toward us.

"I'm going to be in a show down the road, at Pulse." In my fantasy version, I wouldn't be nervous with a cop looking me up and down; I would look forward to the frisk. But here I'm faced with the plain reality of being a man in a wig and skirt, at least by my standards, and I'm not sure what kind of local standards might be viewing me in this part of the country.

Snapshot: Unknown. Two young men grapple on a foam mat, one in a blue Lycra gym suit, the other in red. I recognize the spread legs and suspended balls as that of my lover's high school body growing into itself. I cannot find myself in this picture.

Snapshot: Chicago, Summer 1994. Denim jeans ripped at the knees. An injury on the job. Blood flows from exposed skin. Black dress shoes, out of focus, drift below on hardwoods. I will go back to cashiering once I've documented the incident and cleaned myself up. Antibacterial soap. Iodine. Band-aids.

The 3 x 5 photos were cut into thirds and then taped together in strips, so most of the images are obscured by fragmentation. No thought went into the actual placement of the photos—I let them fall where they might, as random as thoughts and memories emerging and evaporating with no particular scheme or order. The photo-strips were then lined side by side against a length of electrical tape and the entire collection wrapped around my waist. The tape serves not only as an adhesive to my skin but also provides the appearance of a shiny black belt.

I give a short dip in my knees and twist at the waist to steal a furtive glance at the skirt, though now blurred with mobility. Nothing crazy or obscene or, most importantly, incriminating jumps out at me. The charge I expect from this cop eyeing me up and down hits like a toke off creeper weed. The thrill of scandal and paparazzi shudders through me.

I must remember: I remain a man in a skirt and wig on the sidewalk. Given my appearance, the question *am I in trouble?* holds deeper implications than an ordinary stop might warrant. How would he get me to the station on his bike for more questioning? I can see it clearly: the filmstrip wig blowing wildly in the desert winds with my rubber-band arms strapped around the Daddy Copper. Tempting though my fantasy sounds, I decide to take a safer approach and lead the conversation in a different direction. "Can I get my picture taken with you?"

He's a tree of a man, tall and thick like a football player who's put on a few pounds since his glory days of high school. His cheeks redden at the sound of my voice; I make no attempt to disguise its natural male timbre—soft maybe, but certainly not womanly. He sort of nods, more like a bobblehead not sure what to do with himself, his face loose and expressionless. I'm not sure what he expected when he stopped me but he certainly seems surprised, dumbfounded even, by the whole scene. What I wouldn't give to wade in the thoughts swimming through his head.

The women oblige with the camera while me and the bike cop stand side by side, neither of us willing to break the boundary of the other's personal space. He has a gun staring out from his holster. I have my closest friends and family all hanging loosely off my hips.

Snapshot: Two years later at Kansas City's Dixie Belle. Honey Tahini is kissy-facing it, still dolled up in her Lady Bunny wig from the night's revelries. David, to my right, has red-eye. It doesn't help that he's made no attempt to remove his eyeliner. His tongue hangs out a la Gene Simmons. I am in the middle, my face smooth from makeup residue. I have a bottle raised to my lower lip. My eyes lower to the lens, tongue wrapped around the neck of the bottle.

He's quick hoisting himself back onto his motorcycle. I must admit, he's probably one of the most polite cops I've ever met: more blushing boy than gun-toting brawn. He raises a single flat hand against the sky and says, "Take care, have a good night." And with that he rides off without checking any of our ID's.

The women and I glow in the aftermath. Our bodies resound in tingly shivers surfacing with goose bumps. It's the sort of thing I've come to experience when the unexpected collides with the everyday. Not that we are the best examples for upholding any mainstream everyday modes, but certainly none of us saw *that* coming. The moment the cop's bike caroms out of sight, the women both exhale a sigh of relief and tell me they've been tripping balls all afternoon. No wonder they became so quiet, motionless in his presence. If it hadn't been for the camera, they probably would've disappeared altogether. They twitter with laughter and chatter incessantly as we continue our journey. I can tell they're coming down from whatever high they're on, ready to crash someplace soon by the way they keep fussing with their backpacks.

The sidewalk leads us into a more desolate, less trafficked stretch of the city. Pedestrians thin to the random panhandler asking for a light or some change. No one readily acknowledges our appearance. The sun bids farewell as weariness descends upon us.

Snapshot: Kansas City, 1995. Blurry self-portrait of two glassy eyes, one eye cut in two by the frame's edge, and a receding shaved head whitened from overexposure. Eyebrows are missing. Noticeably so. You might mistake me for a terminally ill patient if you didn't know I plucked those brows off all on my own, hair by individual hair.

Edge of the world. We stand in front of what looks like an abandoned building. Windows are boarded and barred. Grated metal gates protect the closed doors behind. A permanent posted sign requests patrons use the side door. The club's name, Pulse, deflates any hopes I'd had for a swanky nightlife given its location. A dead city sunk at the end of the road. No cars or people about. Not even any cops, friendly or otherwise, to be found. Across the street, a run-down hotel squats on the vista, its

Vacancy sign glowing red-orange above empty balconies. Wrought iron railings bend the length of closed doors and draped windows.

The women discuss their options for dinner on the sidewalk while I peek inside the club. I report back, telling them the building's as empty inside as the streets have become outside. Their decision comes as no surprise when they retreat in the direction we came from, where the possibility of people presents a more promising situation—and maybe a clean bed for the night. I tell myself it doesn't matter, though I wonder if I would be better off joining in on whatever adventures wait in store along their path. But I pass over one unknown in favor of another; I stand by this ghost world. I've enjoyed their company while I kept it, had even acclimated myself to their sweaty incense and resin stench, but I'm determined to see my performance through to its end. So we part. Our paths will probably not cross again.

What a relief to finally get into the confines of the club where I can prop myself up on a stool and give my aching feet a rest. The bartender tells me to take my music, a second-generation cassette tape with the words *Which Dreamed It* scrawled in pencil, to the DJ booth.

I fade into the shadows along the outskirts of the dance floor, looking for a place to perch. How I might sit in the photo strip skirt hasn't occurred to me, something I find impossible to do without bending or ripping off some of the photos. The outfit was originally meant to be a quick on and off kind of costume, nothing all-night about it. But with drag time, 8 pm is ten or midnight or whenever the show director damn well feels like it. Anything to make the night last a little longer. I find a nook with a standing tabletop to place my drink: cranberry juice, no ice. Before I can take the stage, a landing strip along one wall of the dance floor—more suitable for an execution than a show—I spend several hours balancing in my platforms.

The ensuing hours pinch my heels into the bottoms of my boots. It can only mean blisters. I give up on my clean tuck in favor of a long piss and a little more comfort than I can afford anywhere else in this costume. The club remains dark and fairly empty. The air smells stale compared to the open landscape I abandoned on the sidewalk. As if the ashtrays haven't been emptied or cleaned, though it sounds like someone might be washing glasses somewhere behind the bar. An occasional laugh accompanies. There's not much for me to do but smoke cigarettes and nurse my drink while mouthing the lyrics to my song over and over. I scan the photos in my skirt to pass the time. Many of the photos are rejects, blurred out of focus or double exposed, but I'm familiar with the images. Even with the cut-up strips, I know the corresponding stories that accompany the photos.

Snapshot: December, 1995. I pose with my boyfriend in front of a Christmas tree made from electrical tape and wire hangers. The tree is covered in silver tinsel and colored lights. I wear a patchwork hoodie and torn jeans. MarBelle is already bundled in his coat, ready to walk out the door. The two of us are just getting over our bout with scabies, which spread through the drag bar where we performed. In the foreground sits the black and white TV casing I turned into a floral arrangement when I outgrew it as a skirt.

Snapshot: Early Winter, Kansas City, 1989. My sisters and I stand in front of my father's casket. Michelle's face is crinkled up like she might be about to sneeze. Kim's lids are heavy, nothing out of the ordinary. She has allergies, she says. My eyes are bloodshot, face fallen. Everyone keeps asking me how I'm doing. I've been drinking with one of Dad's union buddies at home. I tell them I'm fine because I want to believe it.

There's one major difference between the Chicago and Albuquerque performances. In Chicago, I convinced myself once a performance was over it could never be repeated. I had a tendency to throw away costumes at the end of a performance, especially heavy wigs and bulky outfits. Beer bottle skirts. Wings made from vintage album covers. Guitar string chokers. Usually disposed right there in the club. Whereas in Albuquerque, I'm obsessed with recreating and documenting the part of my past I want to remember. I can salvage the best parts of a costume and find ways of reconstructing the leftover materials into something new for future shows—like a photo skirt.

I imagine constructing my outfit using photos taken from the disposable camera I brought along. I could even hang a photo exhibition with what I shoot, except there isn't much audience to be found on this particular night. There are maybe seven people in the whole bar. Not one person has approached me or shown interest in what I'm wearing or so much as looked in my general direction. So I saunter up to the main bar where a couple of regulars are chatting it up with the bartender. They don't smile when I ask for their photo, but I take it anyway.

Snapshot: Kansas City. My mother is hunched over the toilet, elbows to knees, her neck craned toward the doorway shutter. Don't you dare press that button. Her mouth and eyes cinch into a disapproving nose. Never again, she tells me.

I don't know how late it's become when the drag show rolls around. A handful of college kids show up to support a local drag queen, who I assume to be a friend of theirs, but at this point I'm tired of trying to be social and ready to get on with it. Only the two of us are performing for the dozen or so patrons crowded around the main bar.

Kandy Kane lip synchs to *Good Ship Lollipop* in a babydoll dress with a giant sucker she licks and licks and licks. She's either forgotten her words or is obsessed with licking. I prefer to believe the latter. Her friends cheer wildly. I snap pictures from the back of the room, hoping there's enough light in this joint to get a decent exposure.

Moments later, I take the stage. One last photo snaps on the three groupies who remain in the audience, none of whom are standing in the direction of my gaze. I place the camera on the lip of the stage, position my hand in front of me, and freeze in time and place, waiting for the music to cue. The meditation on my hand and the stories that come when I focus on its details—a scar, a crease, the length of my nails—holds me entranced.

Snapshot: Chicago, 1994. A half-eaten pizza, shaped like a crescent moon, sits next to a dirty ashtray beside the papasan couch. Taking a pizza out of the oven requires no oven gloves or hot pads or even a dinner plate because I'm equipped with such long, hard nails. I slide out the pizza hot from the oven and balance it atop my outstretched fingers. Eat the pizza directly off my fingernails. Normally, I will eat an entire frozen pizza in one sitting, leaving only the crumbs on the hardwoods.

Snapshot: Childhood. Bleeding hearts grow wild along the side of the house. My mother works at growing her own flowers in the backyard. Hen and chicks overflow a raised brick planter. Yucca plants sprawl along the border of the patio. I dig alongside Mom with bare hands to see what will come of this year's garden. A scar rests between the knuckles of my index and middle finger, acquired while moving a rock border at my mother's request. I don't remember there being any pain, but the bleeding didn't stop right away. Ended my work for the afternoon. Gardening is not easy work. I've come to prefer the wildness of those bleeding hearts, though it's comforting to know not all scars are confined to tragedies.

Snapshot: Chicago, 1994. As I stare deeply into my hand, waiting for the music to start, some guy from the crowd shouts out, "It's a hand, bitch!" When the music starts I stare him down and snap pictures of him throughout the performance. What I wouldn't give for that kind of audience again.

The shortest drag show in history ends without a fuss. The DJ spins dance music, a welcome change of pace, but I'm already gathering my belongings, taking a final inventory before I walk the long road home. The barback props open the front door as a small band of women enter the club. A cool breeze sweeps through the building. The fresh air and music washes over me, fills me from the bottoms of my boots with unexpected buoyancy. Two of the college boys jump around on the dance floor with glow sticks. They motion for me to join; I have nothing to lose. My heels burn but I don't care anymore. It feels good to be out of the isolation of reverie and back into the flowing vibrancy of the moment.

I spend a good half hour dancing beside a woman with the talkin'est eyes. They twinkle with warm laughter, without her ever uttering a word. Once the college boys are called away to Kandy Kane's entourage, we remain the only two on the dance floor. I'm pleased with my new dance partner. It doesn't matter what song might come up next; we'll dance.

The two of us do a basic version of step-touch, step-touch, circling around each other for slight variance while keeping our eyes in constant contact. Hers eyes radiate hot and spicy brown with a glow like embers smoldering beneath them.

"You're not a woman?"

I shrug my shoulders up and jut my neck forward, eyebrows raised. "No."

"So you're a man?"

"Yes."

"Oh. You're a man, then?"

"Yes."

I wonder if there's more to my new friend than talkin' eyes and a steady rhythm. She reaches out and ruffles my skirt. I'm not sure if she's working to verify something or if she just likes the tactile sensation. Maybe she wants a better look at the pictures. All I can think is that she'll rip a strip off and then I'll be exposed for the walk home. Maybe that's her point. I play coy, continue smiling and moving to the music until my poor feet can't take it any more. I tell her I have to take a break, get some water and put my feet up.

"Ok. But when you're ready, let's keep dancing."

The bartender points me to a side patio where I step outside to cool off. The parking lot glistens with puddles from a recent shower. The plastic chairs are wet as well, and the temperature has dropped considerably. How refreshing to breathe in the fresh, cool air. At this point, I'm not worried about a wet butt and figure the photo paper must do a fairly decent job of repelling water as long as I don't spend too much time lounging. I slide gently into a chair and throw my legs up to rest on another.

I guzzle my water. It doesn't feel like I've rested long enough, I can still feel the heat steaming off the top of my head, but I'm exhausted and don't want to get caught in a downpour walking home. Before I leave, I walk toward the bar to say goodnight to my dance partner. Both arms support me on either side in the doorframe while I survey the bar and dance floor, but she is nowhere to be found. Surely we'll meet again. I give one last, long look before turning for home.

Since night has fallen, the hotel across the way buzzes with new life. A scraggly looking toothless man hollers at me. "Come on up. HEY. Come on, I gotta room." Then someone else whistles from behind. I smile and wave like a fucking homecoming queen, forced to acknowledge anyone who crosses my line of sight, but keep moving. I should be snapping photos left and right but all I can think about is how miserable my feet are in these heels. And my walk, I'm sure, shows it. It's all I can do to keep from limping along but I'm not about to take off my boots with the wet pavement and broken glass. Not to mention I still have an appearance to uphold. What will my fans say at the coffee shop?

As it turns out, hardly a soul's in sight the rest of the way. The Double Rainbow closed hours ago and the rain swept stragglers off the sidewalks for the night. The walk home feels twice as long as it did going out. The chorus to *Which Dreamed It* runs an interminable loop through my head: *And I am the only one / who will undo what's been done / I will not end what's begun / to be / I am / I am...*

I traipse through the front door and pull off my boots first thing. Those boots have always been a little too small, always rubbed terrible blisters on the backs of my heels, but I'm convinced it's all been worth it; the boots are too damn sexy not to wear. I pull down the cardboard box I prepared for packing everything away after the show. Next time I construct this performance, all my needs will be nicely tucked away in a single storage box. *Tres facile.*

Nothing's ever as easy as the first time. The first time has nothing to live up to, nothing to compare itself against; it is what it is, for better or worse. Even though this time has been different—and I know it's been different, I worked at making it different—there remains a residual quality within me that anticipates certain recurrences from the original experience.

Snapshot: Memory. A surge of faces push toward me from the crowd. They want me to come back. Can't wait to see what I might do next. Take my number. Can I buy you a drink?

I can't break free from what has come before. I am left in a strange space of familiarity with this performance, even though I told myself it would not be the same. It would be better. At some point, it's out of my control.

Snapshot: Chicago, 1994. Vikki Spykke invites me to perform with her at Shelter. She'll pay me to be in her show. She tells me she can't wait for me to meet some of the other performers around town. Gina Taye. Boa Boa. Candy Apples. This is the beginning of something big.

Snapshot: Chicago. A local fag-rag included me in their gossip column. They said my untucked genderfuck drag is the future. The future, baby!

Earlier renditions of drag experiences leave traces that tie me down with expectation. Just when I think I'm reaching out for something new, I realize I'm clinging to what has come before. There must be some way of stripping myself from the preconceptions of my past.

I tear myself out of the costume as best I can, careful not to rip the photos. As I start unraveling the skirt it becomes embarrassingly apparent that there are no filmstrips—none at all—along my backside. How long have I been showing my ass? No wonder they were howling like cats in heat on my way home. Come and get it, boys. And that means somewhere, probably in the chair at the bar, personal affectations were left behind for someone else to discover. Will that person care about putting my pieces together? Or simply sweep my history away with the beer bottles and cigarette butts and whatever other kind of rubbish might wash up from the sidewalks? There's a chance no one will even realize I've left something behind.

With everything stuffed into the cardboard box, I shove it all up onto my steel shelving-unit in the corner of the room. At last, I am naked and alone in my apartment. I take a hot shower, standing longer than is necessary to let the water run down my neck and back, scrubbing as much evidence of Evie off my face and head as I can, before I curl up on the futon for the night. I dream about the woman with talkin' eyes. She sleeps with her body pressed against mine, and whispers the names of our children all through the night.

When I wake up in the morning it's raining, hard. I hear rushing water and sit up, rub the sandy grit from my eyes, and adjust to the hazy light of a new day. When I stand up the sound of water gushing sets me into panic mode. I stumble over to the front door, flip the light switch, and stand in awe of the steady stream pouring into all my boxes. A puddle resembling a small lake rises from the corner of the room.

Most of my belongings survive, but all the cardboard boxes and paper material are destroyed. Even so, my world does not wash away so easily. One photo endures.

Snapshot: Fall, Albuquerque, 1997. I stand alone, against a sidewall looking directly into the camera. The frame captures a full body shot, revealing the photo outfit in its entirety. In the background, a man stands at a table directly behind me. He wears a cowboy hat, his body turned sideways, beer bottle pulled to his lips. He looks away from the gaze of the camera, at something in the distance—out of the camera's range.

Nun

Dan Moreau

My apartment building was next to a Catholic girls' school. The school had a basketball court which I played on. The security guard would often shoo me away. A nun who worked at the school would come watch me play and chat with me. She was very friendly. She had a round pale face. Her habit was white, not black like in European countries. She wanted to learn French and for me to teach her. I felt strange giving French lessons to a nun. I felt even stranger talking to her while I sweated and played basketball wearing only shorts and a tank top. But after I talked to her the guard never bothered me again.

But What Did You See?

Myron Michael

one

The streets of San Francisco are soiled. To sleep on them it takes a certain kind of brawn, a certain kind of attitude: *this is where I am so this is where I'll sleep!* Some have it, some don't. Those that are closest to the pigeons don't need it; they navigate the city like sewer rats routing every through way and not a through street; they move like tour guides across area codes around the bottom of knobby hills, towing shopping carts and garbage bags over-spilling with throwaways; they know where to safely make their pallets and hang their underpants to mark their territory. Some are the friendliest tour guides. Others will spit in your face and hurl vulgarities forged like knives in the air. They excrete where they choose and use their hands as tissue to finger paint on federal buildings. Some are artists; some are in need of medical care. Every pigeon flies away from me.

two

His skull cap is black, covers his head entirely, is turned-up at his ears; his dreadlocks are black, thick black ropes of hair hanging above his shoulders; his coat is black, black polyester too short for his arms, is open; his flannel is black with white lines outlining golden squares, is open at his chest; his chest hairs are a nappy bush of black beneath his hand; his hand is open with fat fingers; his fat fingers are scratching his chest; his finger-nails are yellow; yellow fingernails on a swollen hand as if he's been cutting down trees and pulling up roots or fighting off cops and fending off vermin; his legs are thin, are dressed in blue jeans soiled with black grime, and so are his shoes, open-toed, covered in black grime: the kind you find in parks where dogs dig up bones. They stop at his ankles; his ankles, too, are black. He is yawning, his gums are also black and pink inside a checkerboard mouth. He is sitting at a bus terminal; he is yawning.

three

By law, urban camping is off limits. Fines are issued; police are merciless. If they catch you tucked in a sleeping bag, nestled against a trunk, or humping a bush, they'll flash their lights, you'll see their badges, then raise your hands where they can see them. If you're fortunate, you'll get a warning. If not, you'll find yourself in court. In this city it's hard to tell the lawyers from the poets, the poets from the painters, the painters from the grifters, the grifters from the bums. In this city, people are alone or people are in love; people are alone in love in this city. The wind is threatening, pushes anything standing in its way, anyway it blows.

Fish Tale

Kasper Hauser

(Rob Baedeker, Dan Klein, James Reichmuth, John Reichmuth)

Rob

I recently invited a group of my friends to go salmon fishing for my birthday, hoping it would be the kind of raw, nature-based experience that my city peers and I were missing. I imagined *The Deadliest Catch,* that Discovery Channel show where dudes with beards spray the f-word at king crabs, burn each other with cigarettes, and occasionally go tits-up in the Bering Sea.

But our trip would be less hardcore. For starters, the charter boat would embark not from an icy Alaskan harbor but from San Francisco's Fisherman's Wharf, where most of the working anglers have been replaced by caricaturists, rollerbladers, and people who paint themselves silver for money. Also, the weather would likely be sunny, and we'd bring our own sandwiches. The plan was to cook our catch for a dinner party the same night—and maybe even eat it with our hands.

I asked James, John, and Dan to come along. Together we were like the Four Horsemen of the Apocalypse: good friends who like to hang out together, joke around, and go on adventures.

James came to entertain, and John to look for sharks. Dan did not come, and this has since become a source of some tension. I must have invited him, but fishing is just not his thing, which is weird, because he's really into swimming and aquariums. He and his family even have this urban druid vibe going on, and you'd think he'd want to take a greedy "gratitude scoop" from Mother Ocean's womb. It just goes to show that you can lead a hippie to water, but you can't make him pay ninety dollars to go on a boat.

James

We left Fisherman's Wharf before sunrise. It was a brilliant day, the ocean was clear and calm, and we caught a couple of salmon, which it turned out were very docile—almost defeatist—fish. Dan would have probably had a great time, using the offshore amnesty to eat himself sick on "unapproved" foods like ChocoDiles.

One problem with Dan missing the trip is that he tends to have a calming effect on my twin brother, John, who can be a little "conniption-y" (and was once kicked out of an LSAT testing center for throwing a Sausage McMuffin at the wall, *hard*). In the afternoon, my brother got sunburned and seasick, and I heard him warning one of the deck hands that our great grandpa was an admiral.

We later learned that John had eaten too many *churros*, the fried Mexican dough sticks that make you feel real jokey for about eighteen minutes and then drop you into a soul-hole.

Dan was not there to soothe John at the dinner party, either. We cooked the salmon, but everybody just sat around with their mouths open saying, "Doesn't it feel like we're still on a boat?"

I'm thinking Dan *was* invited? But as the only one of us with a wife and kid, he may have used them as a "human shield" to get out of something he didn't want to do. (He pulled the same bullshit with this article, which you'll see when you get to his section at the end: totally phoned in.)

John

Rob's birthday is in September, which is high shark season off the coast of San Francisco. I know a lot about sharks, and have actually studied them—on the Internet, and in the paperback classic *Shark Attacks on Man*—so I was more than happy to share my knowledge with the crew. But these deckhands had a thing against "book smart" people, and if you tangled someone else's line you were an "idiot." When I started talking about great whites, they had a lot of opinions.

There were other reasons why we butted heads. They were drunks, and I don't party anymore, so I both resented and envied them, sort of like a homophobic Marine who finds himself driving by gay bars that aren't on the way home.

And they weren't serious fisherman. If we were on "The Deadliest Catch" together, I would be the deck boss, and they would be the greenhorns who get washed off the boat during the opening credits. As they went under I would say, "Fisherman's Wharf can be a fickle mistress, giving and taking at will."

In the end, my argument with boatswain Randy was basically a clash between blue-collar shark knowledge and white-collar shark knowledge. But it turns out I was right: great whites *do* have jelly filled electro-sensors called the *ampullae of Lorenzini.*

Dan probably would have helped in this situation. He tends to defuse conflicts, and might have redirected the discussion toward aquariums, or maybe said, "You know what? You're *both* right! 'Cuz nature is amaaaaaazing!"

Someone should have invited him.

Dan

I am not a hippie. I gave out homemade Christmas gifts *one* year.
I don't remember Rob inviting me, and while I probably wouldn't have gone fishing, I would have liked to have come to the dinner party. My family was broke at the time, and I would have eaten my newborn son's weight in salmon.

The thing is, life is like that Mr. Deadly Crab show those guys watch: Any time you put a bunch of alpha dudes on a boat, someone's gonna flip out.

Peace ;-)

Travel

Elizabeth Robinson

for Craig Watson

What I most remember is the continuity of remembering,
riding the pleasant coincidence the mind makes.

Serene and fake.

There: a passenger just debarked the boat.

And, here, the water splashes up the lip of the boat
and onto my wrist.

I smell it: "climate in the name of heaven."

Redolent with movement, as scent always is.

You said you were writing about paradise, but also about hell, and so
I remembered both, remembered, especially, the river, Lethe,

quirk of recall

assembled to impart, depart for you.

The Hole in the Adverb

Elizabeth Robinson

The words were pierced through with tidy holes.
A convenience, ultimately,

for it permitted us to thread them on a string. The holes
obeyed the line as they themselves

moved implacably over the infinitely small plane of the string.
So the aggregate becomes a unity. Clutter shaves itself

away. Yet the necklace wraps around the neck, too snugly.
Coherence owes itself to the hidden hollow around which it clusters.

The throat remonstrates. It clears itself, hypocritically.

Interview with Adam Johnson

Fernando J. Pujals

On April 15, 2010, award-winning fiction author Adam Johnson visited San Francisco State University to receive the second annual Gina Berriault Award. Johnson, former Wallace Stegner Fellow and Associate Professor of Creative Writing at Stanford University, is the author of such eccentric, evocative works as *Emporium* (2002) and *Parasites Like Us* (2003). Prior to his guest lecture and reading, I had the opportunity to steal away with Johnson for a lively discussion of his work against the backdrop of perhaps the strangest campus pub in the United States.

14H: How was writing *Parasites Like Us* different from writing your stories, or the novel you're finishing now?

AJ: That was a real transitional piece for me. I had been writing stories about alienation and dislocation. A theme of mine was difficulty making human connections. But then I found the woman of my dreams. And we had kids. And I started teaching creative writing, which is really rewarding and I found my voice as a writer and began to get some of the poison out. Suddenly I wasn't the guy who was feeling dislocated all the time. I felt really connected to many people and many important things in my life. Suddenly all the fuel for my work had been spent. *Parasites Like Us* starts out with a guy, his mom has died, he's all bummed out, his dad is distanced from him, he's not doing well at work. I started with that but I became a different person over the writing of it, and it did come to be about an epic journey of people coming together, about stripping away the unimportant things in life and finding essential relationships and risking it all to make that happen. That was very pure and rare personal experience for me as a writer. To be able to incorporate personally what was happening into the artifice of fiction, on the fly—that can only happen when you're writing to discover.

14H: Would you elaborate on that, the idea of writing to discover?

AJ: If I could just generalize horribly, based on my limited experience in the world of writing, I think there are two kinds of writers. There are people who write outside themselves. They hear about a plane crash in Canada. They think: "I have to write about a plane crash in Canada." So they do some research. They look stuff up, watch a couple YouTube videos, and they knock that puppy out. And it's pretty good! And then there are people like me, whose inspiration comes from some unknown connection with the self. The process is very inward, very based on how I feel, on inspiration. And so those are the slow writers, who allow their narratives to grow and change, to alter course, something that would never happen if you started with an outline.

14H: I read somewhere that you and your wife were married five times? That you had five ceremonies, is that right?

AJ: My wife and I had five weddings. We were married once. We had hoped to have a sixth wedding ceremony in the desert with Target Match pistols in which we would shoot each other in the heart with bulletproof vests on. We were living in LA at the time, and it wasn't as easy to buy body armor over the internet as it is now. We were trying to score some Kevlar. Then the North Hollywood shoot-out happened, and it became illegal to buy body armor for personal use in California. That law later got struck down. Still, we ended up not having that dreamed-of sixth wedding. This probably sounds strange but that was going to be, for my wife and I, our final wedding, our ceremony of ceremonies. But, you know, we've got three kids now and you can't go around shooting your old lady any more.

14H: [laughing] Is that where the story "Trauma Plate" comes from?

AJ: It's interesting about "Trauma Plate." That story came out of the night in which I did a ride-along with the CRASH unit, a gang intervention unit. The two cops I rode with were dressed like soldiers, and they saw I had the same skin color as them and the same buzz-cut as them, and they dropped their guard and decided to be themselves around me. They put a bulletproof vest on me, and we went and started causing trouble for decent and non-decent folk alike. But I have to admit it was infectious, that sense of power. I wasn't the one actually kicking down doors, but doors were kicked, and I had never been in a place where just about any will could be exercised. These two guys felt very comfortable doing anything they wanted. I had to admit there was a sick thrill to that. Someone would say, "Let's pull that car over," and justified or not, they'd hit the lights and siren.

At the end of the shift, we went around to the trunk of the police cruiser. The cops threw all their body armor in. But I just couldn't remove that vest. They kind of looked at me like, "Okay, c'mon we got to close the trunk. Take your bulletproof vest off." I couldn't do it! I had become a person for whom . . . I guess in one night, I became invincible. It sounds like a cliché, but I literally couldn't take that vest off. This cop finally said, "C'mon we got to go." Shame beat out invincibility, and when I peeled off the vest, steam rose from my body. I realized my shirt was drenched. We were in Arizona. They threw it in the trunk and I went home.

In the end, it wasn't about that feeling of power and invincibility that the story became about. The story's discovery was that maybe it was the citizens, and not the police, who needed bulletproof vests. Those were the people who lived in fear. And what of the feeling that I'd had, that a bulletproof vest could save you from anything? So I wrote a story about a young woman who was riddled with fears. She seeks to allay them with a bulletproof vest that she becomes addicted to wearing, but it's the opposite that needs to happen—she needs to drop her guard, embrace the world, because she'll never find love and trust otherwise. In the end she gets her boyfriend to shoot her in the heart. That's the story that made my old lady want me to shoot her, which is really sexy, in my humble opinion.

14H: In that story, and I think in all your stories, there's a sense that the story won't finish until it's really run its course, until it's done its work. Specifically in "Trauma Plate," I get that sense with the shifts in point of view. I wondered if you could talk about the point of view choices you made in the story?

AJ: That first section is in the first person, from the perspective of the father. I love the delusion of the first person. Someone thinks he's telling story X, but he's really telling story Y, and the distance between the two is character. Plus, the reader gets the joy of different stories. "Trauma Plate" was going to be a brief story featuring a father who complained about what the world was coming to, with all its dangers, but at least his own daughter was safe. It was just going to be a four-page story. Then over a couple weeks it haunted me. That guy wasn't making his daughter safe, just the opposite. And I let that dude get away with it! That dude thinks he's being a good dad, but he's not!

So I had to tell the wife's story to counter the father's perspective with another version of events. I tried her story in the first person, but she was resigned, reticent. She had accepted her fate in some way and just wouldn't speak. On instinct I went third person. I had to tell the story for her, to reach in and use a professional narrator to get it out because she never would have shared it. By the time I was done with that I was like, *it's really the daughter's story.*

Suddenly, I didn't care about anything in the world but getting the truth of that young woman. I didn't know that she was going to ask the boyfriend to shoot her . . . I didn't know anything. I just had to get her voice. I tried the first person and the third. They were both not quite right. With the third person it felt like I was taking her story from her. The first person felt like she was bursting; she had this attitude. And then the second person came. It just happened. Sometimes the second person can be the imperative. You're making someone do what they don't want to do. Sometimes the second person is positioning the reader as character. But there's also that 'you' that I love; it's the pronoun we speak to ourselves with, as in "Oh, you've got to quit saying stupid jokes at parties, Adam. They'll think you're an idiot." It's that intimate 'you' that you use to converse with yourself. No one's ever meant to hear it, so it's no confessional or maudlin. It's not asking for the reader's sympathy. In that way, the second person can be very private, and the reader can feel like an interloper in a character's inner terrain. Once I got the daughter's perspective in a way that was intimate and personal, that story became a real portrait of a family. Getting that right meant a whole lot to me.

14H: I noticed in "Cliff Gods of Acapulco" there are two vantages that are kind of fighting against each other. There's the vantage of telling the immediate story, but the one that keeps intruding is the speaker that is beyond this sort of awakening.

AJ: Right, and told from different time frames and different places. You know, I tried to write that piece in the present tense and the past tense, and I needed another past. A deep past. But that was awkward because there were different levels of consciousness in that piece temporally. I had to chart it out to keep track myself but I wrote from five different vantage points, five different places of narration in time. I don't know that the reader could sort them all out, but it worked in my mind. It did feel like it was a very personal story in that way.

I've often felt like I was behind the ball in many ways. You know, I mentioned that my parents didn't tell me they were getting divorced until I came home from school one day and there was a van. A moving van and everything was loaded up. I had no idea that my parents were having trouble. It threw me into a state in which I trusted nothing. I suddenly believed that behind every surface was some wooden falsity. That story ["Cliff Gods of Acapulco"] is a story of the me that's older and knows and understands and a has sense of the big arc of things. The me that's foolishly stumbling along, trying to find my way, turned off and muted. There's a little bit of the innocent me there too. I think people do have chronic issues that are always going be in their work.

14H: When talking about your writing, some people point to what they consider absurd or surreal. But for me, reading them and listening to you now, it seems that the drive still lies in the internal lives of the characters.

AJ: People talk about my work, they say, "It's absurd. You've got a talking bomb robot. People wear bulletproof vests." For me the real absurdity in life has always been emotional absurdity. I published "Teen Sniper" and then next month there's a teenage sniper shooting up DC. I mean, people fly in bathtubs through hurricanes. There's nothing you could try to make up that hasn't taken place in real life. But the idea that two people can love one another and still break up, or that brothers stop talking to each other, or that the parents of a kid get divorced, that is . . . that's incomprehensible to me. That's the real absurdity of life that I can't wrap my head around.

14H: Still, in some way, you wouldn't deny that what people see as 'absurd' *is* in the work. I wondered how things like Clovis people or talking bomb robots free you to deal with those chronic issues you mentioned.

AJ: I see this with some of my students at Stanford, and it's true of me to some degree. With brightness comes awareness and sometimes hyperawareness. I think a byproduct of being super smart is being neurotic, which is you're overly self-aware. If I have my students—and they're all very bright—write free verse, they'll write a line, then they'll reconsider. They'll think, "Oh that's maudlin or sentimental." They can't move a step forward without reconsidering. But, if I give them a sonnet, suddenly their critical minds start counting syllables, doing their ABBA rhyme scheme. They're trying to mark the stresses of iambic meter, and the smart side gets occupied with that. So then, the creative side comes out. Without knowing it they can reveal themselves and be very honest on the page, very naked in a way that they can't otherwise. I do believe to some degree that—now I'm not saying I'm smart—but I do think that my critical, judgmental faculties are occupied by research.

Writing about and researching snipers or the arctic tundra, or the Clovis people, kind of gets one part of my brain going and allows me to access my chronic issues on another level.

14H: Is there anything you just know you wouldn't write about?

AJ: You hear about great writers who, in times of turmoil, were forced to write propaganda for evil institutions so I don't think I could say, under certain circumstances, there's something I wouldn't write. It would have to be something I wasn't interested in.

14H: Do you feel that your writing must achieve some political or moral purpose?

AJ: I've had the chance to see writers at various points in the arc of their careers. You know first decade, second decade, some people write forty, fifty years. I think the farther they get into the relationship with their material, and their sense of themselves as storytellers, the more duty they feel for their work to achieve certain ends and to have a responsibility. To convey something important to the reader. I had a professor, a good professor, who used to ask us, "Why do we write stories? What is the responsibility of the story to its reader?" And I'd say, "C'mon! Stories rock! Stories are awesome! That's why we write them."

14H: And they are.

AJ: Right! But now, like ten, fifteen years later, twenty years later, I *am* asking those questions. Hey, here's my kids having fun in this room of the house, and I'm in this room of the house not paying attention to them. Instead, I'm paying attention to pretend people. Like, this story better be doing something important because I'm missing something important. Once I had kids, I started applying new standards to the application of my time. And what the responsibilities of my words were. I have seen with older mentors, that that's the direction you head. Right now, I still don't, I don't want any politics to get in the way. Politics can cordon off the possibilities of what a character can do and reveal. Right now I wouldn't let that happen, but later I might.

14H: What do you think about someone saying that you shouldn't write about North Korea because you're not North Korean?

AJ: I see people write what I call "Peace Corps" stories. An American, usually a white person, goes into a place in some other part of the world where people aren't white. And they have a profound experience, but it's all through their perspective of discovery. Then they come home and they're like, wow, changed or something, and they're moved to write a story about a person who goes abroad, interacts with a different culture and has a transformative experience. But, um, if you really want to tackle that experience, don't you need to make that empathetic leap of getting to know those people who helped transform you? Why do you need that bridge of a character from your culture? The reader doesn't need the comfort of a familiar tour guide—why does the author? Why not just go do the research, or interview people, talk to people? Go there.

I mean, there are considerations. In terms of politics, people wonder about appropriation. They'd be like, "Hey, who's that dude? He doesn't look so Korean. Why doesn't he stick to his own culture? Who does he think he is to tell the lives of some of the most oppressed people in the world?"

But I don't want to be a writer in a world where you can't make those leaps. I invite my students to write across gender, culture, age lines, and experience lines. Especially in the first person. To speak in the voice of another. You're going to get some of it wrong. I understand that, too. I think also, people will say, oh those are some of the most oppressed people on earth, and appropriating someone else's suffering to get a book out of it, why not do nonfiction to do justice to them? I believe that fiction can lend a dimension of humanity, of psychology, that nonfiction sometimes can't. It can get to the heart of something.

The Greatest North Korean Story Ever Told
from The Orphan Master's Son

Adam Johnson

Citizens, come, gather round the loudspeakers in your kitchens and offices for the sixth installment of *The Greatest North Korean Story Ever Told*. Have you missed an episode? They are available for playback in the languages lab of the Grand People's Study House. When last we saw the coward Commander Ga, he had been treated to his own Tae Kwan Do demonstration by the Dear Leader! Don't be fooled by the Commander's dashing uniform and cleanly parted hair—he is a tragic figure, who has far, far to fall before talk of redemption can begin.

For now, our dazzling couple is crossing Pyongyang late after an opulent party as, neighborhood by neighborhood, substation power switches are being thrown to cast our sweet city into slumber. Commander Ga drove with exuberance and fatalism, while Sun Moon leaned with the turns in a numb, obligatory way.

"I'm sorry about your movie," he said.

She didn't respond.

He looked at her, staring not ahead, but to the side, at the dark buildings they passed.

He said, "You can make another one."

She dug through her purse, and then in frustration closed it.

"My husband never let me run out of cigarettes, not once," she said. "Every morning, there was a fresh pack under my pillow."

The Pyongchon eating district went dark as they drove through it, and then one, two, three, the housing blocks along Haebangsan Street went black. Nighty-night, Pyongyang. You earned it. No nation sleeps as North Korea sleeps. After lights out, there is a collective exhale as heads hit pillows across a million households. When the tireless generators wind down for the night and their red-hot turbines begin to cool, no light glares on alone, no refrigerator buzzes dully through the dark. There's just eye-closing satisfaction and then deep, powerful sleep filled with dreams of work quotas fulfilled and the embrace of reunification. The American citizen, however, is wide awake. You should see a satellite photo of that confused nation at night—it's one grand swath of light, glaring with the sum of their idle, indolent evenings.

Lazy and unmotivated, Americans stay up late, engaging in television, homosexuality and even religion, anything to fill their selfish appetites.

The city was in full darkness as they drove by the Hyoksin subway's Ragwan station. Their headlights momentarily illuminating an eagle-owl atop the subway's vent shaft, its beak at work on a fresh lamb. It would be easy, dear citizen, to feel for the poor lamb, plucked so young from life. Or the mama sheep, all her love and labor for nothing. Or even the eagle-owl, whose duty it is to live by devouring others. Yet see that this is a happy story, citizen: by the loss of the inattentive and disobedient lamb, the ones on other rooftops are made stronger.

They began making their way up the hill, passing the Central Zoo where Dear Leader's own Siberian Tigers were on display next to the pen that housed the zoo's six dogs, all gifts from the former king of Swaziland. The dogs were kept on a strict diet of soft tomatoes and kimchi to lessen that animal's inherent danger, though they would become meat-eaters again when it came time for the Americans to visit!

In the headlights they saw a man running from the zoo with an ostrich egg in his hands. Chasing him up hill with flashlights were two watchmen.

"Do you feel for the man hungry enough to steal?" Commander Ga asked as they drove by. "Or for the men who must hunt him down?"

She spoke, "Isn't it the bird who suffers?" she asked.

The cemetery was dark, as was the fun faire, the gondola chairs hanging pure black against a blue-black sky. Only the botanical gardens were lighted. Here, even at night, work on the hybrid crop program continued, the precious seed vault protected from an American invasion by a grand electric fence. Ga glanced at a cone of moths, high in protein, circling in a security light, and a sense of urgency came over him as he drove slowly up this last stretch of dirt road.

"Look," he said. "I came into this world with nothing. I pretended that I had parents, friends, I saw the other orphans as brothers, like we were a big family, but we weren't. And now I've been given this portrait of everything I never had. It's an illusion, I know it. You're right, this car is not mine, it's a prop from a movie. But even if it's not real, I feel the road, I'm driving it. You, you're not mine, Sun Moon, but you're beside me, and I feel your heart large and hurting. Maybe this isn't real, but I'll take it, I'll take the illusion."

"You have to understand," she said. "I wished my husband gone a thousand times—*if I could just snap my fingers and make him disappear*, you know how many times I had that thought? But tonight, in there, I missed him. When I was with him, I knew that no harm would ever come to me. At these dinners, I was free to laugh and gossip. But if he's gone, if he wasn't safe, I guess tonight it sunk in what that meant for me, how I'd been living a fantasy. My husband tested his masculinity every single day, and now he's gone."

Here, Commander Ga pulled up before the house. They were home. And now off to sleep, the two of you . . .

Oh, Sun Moon, our heart never stops going out to you!

Let us all repeat together: We miss you Sun Moon!

Finally, citizens, a warning that tomorrow's installment contains an adult situation, so protect the ears of our littlest citizens as the actress Sun Moon decides whether she will open herself fully to her new husband Commander Ga, as is required by law of a wife or whether she will make a misguided declaration of chastity.

Remember, female citizens, however admirable it may be to remain chaste to a missing husband, such a sense of duty is misplaced. Whenever a loved one disappears, there is a bound to be a lingering hurt. The Americans have the saying, "Time heals all wounds." But this is not true. Experiments have shown that healing is hastened only by self-criticism sessions, the inspirational tracts of Kim Jong Il and replacement persons. So when the Dear Leader gives you a new husband, give yourself to him. Still: We love you Sun Moon!

Again: We love you Sun Moon!

Show your verve, citizens.

Repeat: We admire you Sun Moon!

Yes, citizens, that's better.

Louder: We emulate your sacrifice Sun Moon!

Let the Great Leader Kim Il Sung himself hear you in heaven!

All Together: We will bathe in the blood of the Americans who came to our great nation to hurt you!

But, we get ahead of ourselves. That is for a future episode.

Featured Artists

◊**Jon Stich** has been creating pictures since he was nine years old, when his father took him to a Red Lobster and he scrawled all over the menu. The first person to be bothered by his artwork was his seventh grade math teacher Mr. Schaffsma, who became angered by Jon's decision to use the back of another student's test to draw a detailed rendition of a gentleman enthusiastically pooping. Since that pivotal moment, he has somehow managed to create and sell artwork of the same quality to the masses. Some of his clients include *Adult Swim, Businessweek*, Yahoo! Personals, *The Source, Vibe, The San Francisco Chronicle, Under the Radar, Adbusters, Heeb, Hyphen Magazine, The Bay Area Alternative Press, Literacyhead*, and DIESEL, A Bookstore. A 2004 graduate of the California College of the Arts, finishing with distinction, he lives and works in lovely Oakland, CA. www.jonstich.com

◊**Dena Schuckit** is a printmaker/painter who was a master printer at Crown Point Press in San Francisco for twelve years before moving to London. Online news is often accompanied by entire slide shows of photos capturing the drama and dynamism of the disaster and the surprising and unplanned landscape that is the deconstructed physical manifest. Schuckit works from stacks of saved and categorized photos pulled from online news sources. Collecting and sorting these pictures is Schuckit's way of mapping her relationship to her landscape. Pattern, shape, color, and event overlap and repeat in a rhizome charting the ebb and flow of civilization vs. nature. Schuckit paints from the connections she finds in the process of organizing piles of collected photos, decontextualizing the subject action from any one specific event. www.denaschuckit.com

◊**Damon Soule** (cover artist) As a child, Damon became so engrossed with drawing that it became a distraction. He dropped out of school opting for the immediacy of a GED, and enrolled in the San Francisco Art Institute. In 1996, Soule became Art Director and Co-founder of FIT Skateboards and Civilian Clothing. After a number of years, he sold his portion of the business to pursue art full-time. Soule's paintings and drawings have been featured in numerous exhibitions in New York, Seattle, Santa Monica, and Rome. Recent solo shows include Thinkspace Gallery (Los Angeles, 2010), and Fecal Face Gallery (San Francisco, 2009). www.damonsoule.com

The Abnormalities of Trevor and Ammie / Jon Stich
acrylic and pencil on illustration board

The Existential Crisis / Jon Stich
acrylic and pencil on illustration board

Realizing the Far-Fetched Sea / Jon Stich
acrylic and pencil on illustration board

Aerial Event / Dena Schuckit
acrylic on wood

Aerial Event 2 / Dena Schuckit
acrylic on wood

Flap / Dena Schuckit
acrylic on wood

Fray / Dena Schuckit
acrylic on wood

Green Smoulder / Dena Schuckit
acrylic on wood

[Without a Body]

Maxine Chernoff

mechanical arms

brass libido

tattooed intention

clear as the image

of Jesus she sees

on the underpass wall

including song

requires a voice

makes bone offer up

sinew and rib

incompletion challenged

without Mrs. Lear

he wanders a ghost

the seasons enacting

their neutrality

[Without Outrage]

Maxine Chernoff

fetish fair jockeys

hollyhock thieves

an architecture

in place of grace

seasons fleshed

in stone

rubbed clean

on edges of water

reading makes

visible

all enunciation

proving seditious

to tongue and ear

strict shores part

[Without Objectivity]

Maxine Chernoff

the hundred voices

electric vibrato

dust of dead bees

and language

human progress

overcome by lullabies

solo of entropy

interrupted by desire

stunted purchase

tethered to music

all about you

Larpers

Steve Gronert Ellerhoff

Venturing into the seeded summer grass behind Hoffman Middle School, a sack of cat food under arm, Mr. Haller sought one kind of movement in the dark and found another. It took a moment for his eyes to adjust. Those shimmering black sticks, bobbing back and forth in agreeable conversation, were katana swords. Two unlit figures, huddled low, wielded them. While he knew kids got up to mischief on the back lawn late at night, nothing he'd ever glimpsed over the fence from the kitchen window led him to believe they were toting Japanese weaponry. It was a neighborhood of family lawyers, comptrollers, and gastroenterologists—not hoodlums.

They wore full samurai battle dress. Homemade, by his reckoning, the tape seams evident. Rigid, rectangular plates shielded their shoulders, chests, and thighs like pangolin scales, the emblem of a green oak tree on both breastplates. Only one donned a helmet, shiny in the night with sweeping sides and two pointy ears, black synthetic fur with white felt insides, poking out of its crown. The wearer, turning to look at Mr. Haller, wore an orange rubber dog nose, affixed with an elastic string, and face paint: black in the pits of his eyes, orange from forehead to cheekbones, and white from there to chin. His friend had a cartoon mouse snout, tipped with a black olive nose, and gray and brown streaks radiating from the center of his face. He wore a hoodie, completely impractical in the humidity, cinched tight with row upon row of brown foam spikes jutting out of it. In each of their swordless hands, triangular sandwich halves.

" 'Ark," the pointy samurai hailed in Dick Van Dyke cockney, "a lone wanderer, my liege!"

The other took a bite from his sandwich. Relieved at encroaching upon thespians instead of armed junkies, Mr. Haller nevertheless backed away.

"Good sir, do you take us for thieves?" The spiky guy withdrew his scabbard and sheathed the sword with a *shumf*. Tossing his sandwich crust, he said, "We'll do thee no 'arm."

He hesitated.

They both raised their painted eyebrows.

"The last hour or so did either of you see a cat?"

"Is that what brings you to 'Offman Prairie?" He went on as though it were natural to butcher the accent. "Methoughts you'd snuck 'ere to eat your kibble in private." He pointed to the cradled bag of cat food.

"Oh. No." Mr. Haller gave the sack a loud shake and squinted over the grass, hoping for the arc of a tail. "He usually comes when I do this at home."

"We've seen a thousand cats in our day!" the mum one said, speaking in a feral Scottish tone. " 'Twas a blasted cat what put us in this grave imposition!" The gruff samurai snorted his doggish snout and returned to his sandwich.

"Dear oh dear, you must excuse 'Is Majesty," the other defended. "Ever since's kingdom was usurped by the vile Cleo, self-proclaimed Empress of Des Moines, 'e's all but retreated into 'imself. 'E won't speak, won't sleep. Indeed, those just now was the first words 'e's spake all night. All I can get 'im to sup on are peanut butter and pickle sandwiches."

Nothing catlike moved in the expanse behind the school, July's grass stilled. "What're you guys supposed to be anyway?"

"By rights I am a duke!" he bragged. "Macduff Scroggins, Duke of Ashworth. And this broken fellow, this forlorn creature full of misery and woe, is the anguishing, exiled, spit-upon, and straggling rightful King of Greenwood."

Ashworth was the municipal swimming pool down at the base of Greenwood Park, several blocks east, behind the Des Moines Art Center. Noticing the way the king's tail bushed orange before terminating in white, he made an educated guess. "So he's a fox. But I can't—are you a porcupine?"

He flinched, his foam spikes bristling. "It's impolite to draw attention so blatantly to another's species."

"Sorry."

"Not to worry," Macduff genuflected. "I don't take thee for a specist. Mayhaps ye've not come 'cross our kind afore. 'Is 'Ighness is indeed a fox. My kind, on the other 'and, is an erinaceous sort, native to other lands. I left the gardens and 'edgerows of Britain when but an 'oglet, riding the swan road to this spacious-skied, amber-waved land. Oft am I mistaken for my cousins, the porcupines, but in truth I am an 'edge'og."

"Well," he said, "great costumes. You part of a club or is it just you guys?"

"Costumes? What club?"

"According to a greater king than I, rest his soul," the fox king growled like Connery, "someone said that the world's a stage and each of us plays a part...."

"Be that as it may," Macduff pondered, "what part are you playing, good sir?"

"I'm just trying to find my daughter's cat. It ran out when I checked to see if I'd left the garage door up."

" 'Ad you?"

"No."

"A second guesser," the hedgehog noted.

"Aye, and educated. He bears the Hawkeye crest." The king referred to the University of Iowa Alumni Association t-shirt he wore.

" 'Oo's ever seen a beakless, featherless 'awk? I've not." He scrutinized Mr. Haller's very being. "Well then? What are ye?"

For an instant he considered playing along. He considered telling them he was a cowboy, No-Name Haller: Colt-wielding knight of the high plains, a character he'd been as a boy on afternoons after school, all through summers. The exhumed hero surprised him. He'd not thought on the drifter from Driftweed, USA, in decades. But he settled for the truth. "I'm a bureaucrat."

"And whereabouts is your burrow, Mr. Crat?"

"What? No, I'm a bureaucrat. In the insurance industry."

"Ah! You toil in the tower at the 'eart of the city?"

"I'm with their competition actually."

"Gentlemanly competition, no doubt! Ye, sir, are a gentleman."

"Thank you."

"By what name doth thee wish to be known?"

Annoyed with their persistent invitation to the land of make-believe, he meant to say Lawrence, Larry being reserved for friends and esteemed colleagues, which these twenty-year-olds weren't, and he couldn't be sure if it was due to their youth or his inability to grasp what the hell they were up to, but, on the spot, he introduced himself as: "Mr. Haller."

The fox leveled a vivisecting eye at him, his glance as sharp as the mall-bought katana sword in his gloved paw, but the Duke offered up respect with a hand flourish. "Well, Mr. 'Aller, 'Awkeye, gentleman, and bureaucrat, by what name might we know your cat?"

"It's my daughter's cat," he clarified. "Mackerel. She named it Mackerel. And I have to find it tonight."

"Might this Mackerel," the King ventured, "be tabby in paternation?"

"Yes!"

"Marmalade in coloration?"

Now they were toying with him, neither the King nor the Duke having the decency to rise from the grass and volunteer simple information. What with it being late and his daughter scheduled to arrive in the morning after a year abroad, he was in no mood. "Look, which way did it go? Just give me that."

The King tilted his snout and jerked a line towards the school.

"He went that way?" he asked. "Thanks a lot." Mr. Haller flip-flopped up the hill to Hoffman, giving the bag of kibble another violent shake.

"Oh, but good Mr. 'Aller," Macduff called, hopping to his feet and following, "we should like to help you find this Mackerel!"

"No, really, thank you," he urged, wanting nothing more to do with them. "Good night!"

They followed. Through the parking lot, around the uninspired, two-story brick building, he headed east on Grand Avenue, past the large houses decades older than the school. His eyes hopscotched along street, yards, and the patches of streetlit sidewalk. The King and Duke traipsed several paces behind, tiptoeing from shadow to shadow like Looney Tunes characters, Macduff trilling out, " 'Ere kitty, kitty!"

Passing the Jewish Reform temple, he pondered its dome and the two-story loggia over the entrance. He'd never been inside. When was the last time he'd even walked by? Was probably pulling Emily in the old wagon, that's how long it must have been. One block from home and full of mystery. He recalled, too, when the temple was desecrated by a couple of teenage Neo-Nazi wannabes. What, fifteen years ago. They'd spray-painted red swastikas on the stone—he saw it on the six o'clock news. And what'd the Jews do? They rehabilitated the kids who'd done it. He'd nearly forgotten that whole deal.

Retrospect made these samurai kids look like the Junior Woodchucks. When he was a teenager, he'd spent his free time masturbating or laboring over a diorama of his own dreamt-up Wild West town: Driftweed, USA. There was a place he'd not visited in a long time. Its remnants, dismantled and boxed, were lost when his mother's basement flooded in the Eighties.

"Might ye bear any relation to a certain Emily Haller?" the King inquired at his elbow.

"She's my daughter." He stopped and searched the idiot's painted face, wondering if he might recognize one of her acquaintances lurking beneath the colors. She'd only ever brought two boys home, each only a couple of times. "You know her?"

"I shared some classes with her at Castle Roosevelt," he claimed, his sword resting at a backward tilt between his helmet and shoulder guard. "A kind lass. And keen, our deserved valedictorian."

"Thank you."

"I take it she's well?"

"She's been teaching English in Japan for a year. I said I'd take care of her cat, and she's back tomorrow, and," he winced, "you know the rest. Listen, who are you so I can say I saw you."

"Lear Hornbuckle," the fox said, so serious. "King of Greenwood."

A caterwaul rent their exchange. Across the street, galloping down a driveway with back arched and tail stiff, Mackerel made like his namesake fleeing a shark.

"Your cat!" Mr. Haller held the food at his shoulder and watched it run down the opposite sidewalk, not stopping, in full retreat. "The hell's got into him?" he asked, gawping as Mackerel sprinted back into the night. "He's a house cat but criminey…"

"I do believe that fiend was molesting your Mackerel." The Duke pointed to the yard it had fled. Two yellow-green eyes flashed at the base of a sugar maple and a raccoon the size of an English bulldog cast a cautious look before hesitating to the trunk's dark side.

He rolled the mouth of the bag tight and socked the bottom with closed fist. The samurai stood with him on the sidewalk, adopting his angst with groans of their own, though it was his alone to bear. A flight of fancy for them was a failing for him, his promise to his daughter broken. It occurred to him that perhaps Mackerel had the right idea in taking off like that from the raccoon, that he should forfeit the search himself and flee the costumed geeks for his side of the bed and Mrs. Haller's whimperful sleep. But that wouldn't bring the cat home, and leaving the side door open a crack should it decide to resurface was out of the question, what with armed drama flunkies roaming the neighborhood.

"It's illegal to run around in public with a blade longer than a couple inches," he said. "Pretty sure about that."

King Hornbuckle sheathed his sword. "Mr. Haller, the situation is more grave than you can know. Your daughter's feline, at last bearing, was prancing straight for my stolen kingdom. The pet entrusted to your care, which can't defend itself from common raccoon ilk, is bound for the claws and paws of that wretched, power hungry tigress—Cleo—and once she has him in her clutches, he, like those wooded acres I once ruled, will be hers."

Mr. Haller scowled and crossed Grand Avenue at an agitated clip, his flip-flops slapping his soles. "The damn cat's coming home with me."

"To Greenwood!" they cried, taking up the rear and brandishing their swords anew.

The Art Center, five blocks from his house, was not a place Mr. Haller visited. From the westward approach, its three stories of curving, moon-white modernist geometry had always struck him as being too sterile, too dental for a building meant to house fine art. Inside its walls, amongst other pieces, were Hopper's lone woman staring into her coffee cup at the automat, Bacon's blood-spattered Pope screaming silently on his throne of terror, a trio of vacuum cleaners stacked in a Plexiglass case by Koons. Behind the museum bloomed a rose garden that sloped down to Greenwood Park, a lagoon, and Ashworth pool. Perfect places for daily strolls never taken.

Gambling on Mackerel's bearing, he entered the museum's driveway, walking by a cast metal sculpture that he'd never contemplated when driving by before: a twelve foot tall animal pyramid of five antlerless caribou, supporting eight deer, supporting four hand-standing foxes. Passing cautiously, as if it were finger-draped warning statuary outside a shrine built on human sacrifice, Mr. Haller resisted the urge to call out the cat's name, kept the bag of food in the crook of his arm unrustled. A paved pathway led around the back of the museum, which changed to Brutalist exposed concrete, the work of another architect altogether, meant to be a big name in circles totally foreign to him. Under hundred-year-old oaks, the rose garden opened up and with it the sound of unsanctioned festivity. He considered crossing the grass to get a peek from behind an eight-foot-tall egg-shaped cairn, but a row of hedges was closer. The King and Duke sneaked along with him.

Beyond, lined with limestone benches and pillars, lay a stone path to a circle segmented symmetrically into beds of red and white roses. Two mossy, hipped roof garrets stood at the far end. At the bull's-eye stood a sundial atop a bronze snapping turtle, and around it thronged what could have been a community college rehearsal of *Cats*.

Maine Coon and calico, ocelot and panther, a dozen breeds for a dozen revelers. Their faces made up, tails trailing in dance, the cats wore tights and leotards, tufted at cuff and ankle. Their forms outlined in the dark, the mewing co-ed coven twirled in song around their obese, bobbleheaded mascot. She sat upon a buckling aluminum lawn chair, glowing white with fur, black stripes marking her rolling sides. Her head, of hydrocephalic proportions, bore a face frozen in psychotic glee. Cartoon eyes, with eyelashes and lavender lids lolling, stared over a down-pointing triangle nose and a grinning mouth curved full with Gorgon fangs. More stripes capped her ears and wrapped around her wispy cheeks.

"Cleo," Macduff grumbled. "So-called Empress of Des Moines…"

An Egyptian Mau, spotted and whorled, strode to the center and thrust her arms high, a real cat in her grip. Mackerel. Holding him at the pits so his hind legs hung, she presented him to their corpulent leader.

Mr. Haller snorted and walked out to face them.

"No, don't!"

He entered the game like a referee, chin high and fearless. "Put the cat down," he ordered from the path.

The cat people broke from song and choreography, spinning low and meeting him with hisses and bared claws. The Egyptian Mau pulled Mackerel to her breast, the cat scrambling against her and vaulting into Cleo's lap. Its claws sunk in, the Empress's thighs quaked, the lawn chair nearly gave. When she settled, his daughter's cat took note of Mr. Haller's arrival. Unaffected by his keeper's brash attempt at rescue, the tabby eased its haunches and relaxed under the Empress's paw.

"Time out, kids." He held his palm out. "Look, you can go back to your little play or whatever you're doing in a minute. I just need that cat."

They peered up at him, mostly girls but a few young men in the clowder, all of them wearing cat iris contact lenses. Naturally, it was a blue-eyed Siamese who thrust her whiskers in the air and spoke for everybody. "All who wish to address Empress Cleo's court," she said, striding to her Empress's side, "must first pledge allegiance to her glorious empire."

" 'Kay, I'm not here to interrupt your dress-up. I'm really just here for the cat." He stepped over some attendants only to be blocked by others.

Cleo waved a paw and they all hushed. A faint muffled mew came from her enormous, team mascot head, the dark-faced Siamese holding her cat-ear headband close to the awful grimace before stretching and translating. "The Empress wishes to know who and what you are."

"No, see, I've been through all that crap already with your friends." He wrung the folded mouth on the sack of cat food. "That's my daughter's cat, and if you don't hand it over, I'll be calling the police!"

"This cat has no name around its neck, no number to call," she said, falling to her knees and scratching under Mackerel's chin. "It's ours to keep and raise as our prince."

"Oh for crying out loud, it's a house cat! The damn thing's never been outside but for the vet."

Cleo drew a circle in the air. The Siamese listened to her instructions. "The Empress wishes to know about these friends you mention. Have you come alone or were you put up to this?"

At the end of the path, brandishing themselves from the hedges, the King and Duke charged the crowd with their swords high over their heads. "Bonzai!"

"Insurgents!" the cats squealed, suddenly wielding what looked like small bags of potpourri. These they lobbed at the samurai, launching salvos and shouting, "I summon forth fire!" or "I summon forth ice!" or "I summon forth lightning!"

Worried the samurai might start swinging their posturing blades, Mr. Haller lunged through the furries and made a swooping grab for Mackerel. The tabby bolted, causing him to sock the white tigress in her protruding belly with the sack of food. A brief wobble and her chair collapsed.

"The Empress!"

They barraged him with spells, organza pouches pelting his chest and shoulders. He squinted, forearms up, blenching at each strike. When one hit his temple, Mr. Haller roared. He forgot, blessedly, what he was. In this moment, he wasn't a husband of twenty-six years or a father to a grown woman or even a senior claims adjuster. He was the outlaw No-Name Haller, bounty hunter from Driftweed, USA, prepared to do anything to haul in that damned cat alive, and this was a balls-out shootout, a real Kilkenny catfight. No mercy! Every buckaroo for himself! He tore the sack open and grabbed fistfuls of kibble, pitching it like gravel, aiming for feline faces.

They shrieked.

He thrilled.

The kibble ran out.

Mackerel had disappeared in the flurry of tights and tails. So had his right flip-flop. Neither resurfacing in the fray, and out of ammo, he made for the trees, dashing on unlevel feet from the pouch and kibble-strewn roses to mown park grass. They let him go catawamptiously chawed up, throwing one last volley, two pouches whispering past and one hitting his left love handle with a beany thud. He took safety behind an oak and, sweating and breathing hard, spied back through the shadows. The fat girl in the tiger costume was still on the ground despite three friends' efforts to tug her onto her hind legs. The rest of the pounce focused on quelling the King and Duke's uprising, both of them cackling fiercely, drawing their enemies to the cairn for their sword-shaking stand. The fox and the hedgehog were in it till the end. Mr. Haller was not.

He cursed the cat and walked back to Grand Avenue and on past the Jewish temple, every other step off balance. Careful as to where his bare foot touched gritty pavement, soft as it was from fifty years in comfy shoes, he carried the shredded scrap of the food sack with him. Rounding the middle school's parking lot, he gave it an empty shake for the hell of it. Something jostled in the one corner left intact. He reached in and pulled out an orange organza pouch. It was packed tight and tied with red ribbon. He picked the knot loose, spread it in his palm. Birdseed. They beaned him with birdseed. He scattered it in the Dean of Students' parking spot and dropped the square of fabric as if it were a hanky meant to draw one's attention.

At the calf-high grass behind Hoffman, he kick stepped down the hill toward his backyard. When he was close enough, he removed and boomeranged the flip-flop at his fence. It fell short.

"Mr. Haller!"

Lear Hornbuckle, dethroned and disgraced King of Greenwood, came running across the parking lot, more equine than vulpine in his boot-clopping approach. He leapt into the grass, scabbard swinging at his side and helmet cupped upside down in his hands. In its bowl, posing with back straight and ears flat like the star of a motorcade, rode Mackerel.

"I surrender this creature to your care, kind sir." His fox snout dangled from its elastic string around his neck.

He was incredulous, the one time he'd ever been happy to see the cat.

"Your maneuver depleted their magic. We had enough resist magic potions to hold them off. Greenwood's ours again thanks to you!"

"Well…"

"Accept the return of this litter-boxer as token of our deep appreciation for your valor on the battlefield." He thrust the helmet forward.

Neither Mr. Haller nor Mackerel wanted to touch each other. After a stuttered attempt, he was able to get one hand on the cat's shoulders and the other under its ribs, pulling it from the helmet and straightjacketing it to his chest. "Thanks. Really. To the hedgehog, too."

"Our appreciation is mutual." The fox seated his sweeping samurai helmet on his head and refastened his nose. "And your daughter. Would you be so kind as to pass on a hello from Jeff Jenkins?"

"You bet, Your Highness."

The King of Greenwood walked away, slapping his thigh guards clean as he climbed the hill toward the school. Before he crested, Mr. Haller was already behind his fence, his fingers dug firmly into Mackerel's scruff.

Weightless, as Children,

Jane Hilberry

as if the whole world were a trampoline, each step as much up as down, as if we might escape gravity, might land on rooftops, be seen rising past windows. Though one of us hung over the railing of the tennis court tower and could have fallen, she didn't, and we were bouncing, slow motion, and landing, and rising, slow motion, and landing, our legs were tall enough to stride streets to the candy store, to step over the crossing-guard with her whistle, her sound a wisp underneath us, nothing to stop us buying candy—strips of taffy in waxed paper, Pixy Stix in red, yellow, blue straws we would suck soggy—we could stride to the library, bring the books home on our heads, as if they were sugar cubes, or boxes for the tiny glass animals we saved our money and bought at the downtown store where every creature had a fragile wing or leg, where glass ducks glided on mirrored ponds. There were no parents, no such thing as after-dark, the evenings were always, and twilight lasted. We moved like animals through the neighborhood or like geese flying over, we didn't live where we lived, we were too large, our steps whole blocks, over houses, our bodies light as balloons. We didn't know what was coming, breasts and well, yes we did have an inkling, the short curly hairs on the edge of the tub where adults had bathed, we hated them, washed them away, we fit together in the tub, splashed water over the edge and angered the father, we went to lakes, larger, where we could swim, our legs reaching into marshes, touching cattails, the murky bottom. We were water skeeters, many-legged, we were the song of frogs in the cattails, and the fluffy seeds of the cattails breaking down, and we were the white of the clouds against the solid song of blue, and we were all of it and none of it, we were the evening wind drying the swimmers leaving the lake, we were the sandwiches in the picnic basket, we were the ants eating the sandwiches, we were peanut butter and marshmallow fluff, we were ice cream running down the sides of the softening cone we were in the backseat with a towel under us, the window open and we were the breeze through the window and the sand in the seats of our suits and our legs not quite touching the floor of the car.

The Memory Game

Alice Pero

for my mother

In the memory game
you have to memorize
where the owl and fish are,
your brain cells reexamined
by the very best authorities
In another test you are asked
to spell "world" backwards
No one blinks when you cannot
think in reverse
or spin the world on its axis
No one has been interpreting your dreams,
but they are making sure your brain is medicated
every four hours, a mind-freeze preventing
seizures or possible escape
You have not yet forgotten my name,
but you inquire for the third time,
"Where do you live?"
I tell you I live with the owl and the fish
and you laugh, reminding me
that you named me after the little girl
who fell down the rabbit hole.

from Fine Creature
a novel

Jackie Corley

Jack got himself locked away in center city Philadelphia. I went to college a few miles outside the city so we know the place. Whether he can tell you anything about that now is something else. He was visiting me at school and we hit all-you-can-eat sushi at Aoi before getting drunk at Finnegan's. We didn't make the connection to 30ᵗʰ Street Station because Jack gave all his money to a con begging for SEPTA fare and then had to piss on the chain-link fence of this fine institution to mark the occasion.

I've never been inside before. Never had a reason to be. Security sends me through the metal detector and then pats me down. They give me a visitor's pass and make me surrender my driver's license before pointing me toward reception. I get a pamphlet on how to deal with the recovering patient. It tells me important things like, "Your friend or family member may be emotionally volatile. He or she may display a self-centered attitude or lack of empathy." That's a tattoo-worthy warning label.

A sign by the elevator says the ward nurse and the doctor on duty have to sign off on any ward leaving hospital grounds. Nobody's going to make a break with one of their charges, nobody wants to bring the crisis home, but the staff isn't taking any chances. A bird could shit on one of those patients; all of Philadelphia could come tumbling down on their soft, pretty heads.

Jack's mother, Regina, said the hospital was the best in the Northeast. It's as antiseptic and white as any other I've been to. There are canopies above the beds—that's the only difference I can see. Regina's asleep on a chair by the window with Jack's old Super Mario Bros. comforter covering her. Her curly hair is knotted and sticking up at odd angles. Tabloids and celebrity magazines are stacked up on the vent next to her. One has fallen from her hand onto the ground.

There are a dozen "Get Well Soon" cards on a piece of twine tacked on the wall under the television. I can't think of any of Jack's friends as Hallmark types, but I wonder if his fiancée (ex-fiancée?) Dani is somewhere on this thread. I finger open each card. The scrawl is neat, feminine. The cards are addressed to Jack but carry long notes to Regina from her coworkers and neighbors. Dani's not in any of these, but neither am I. I guess it shows what the two of us are worth.

"I told him already," Regina says. I pull my hand back from the string of cards, startled, and turn to face her. Regina's eyes are still closed. She's babbling in her sleep. "He doesn't want sausages."

The woman could sleep through the apocalypse. Jack and I used to find her like this on her throne at the kitchen table. When we got bored in Red Bank, we would go to Jack's house to torture poor Regina. We'd grab thick clumps of her hair and hairspray it straight up. We'd take one of her lipsticks and draw bright red circles on her cheeks. I would bury my face in one of the laundry piles on the floor to keep from howling and waking her up.

When Regina stumbled into semi-consciousness she was a beast. There was nothing gentle or warm in her like daytime Regina. Her eyes would be red and glossy, half-closed, and she'd glare up at Jack and say, "I know what you're planning. I know what you're hiding from me." It would be too much for me and I would fall back on the kitchen floor, kicking my heels on the linoleum. "You'll be the next one. Just wait. He's got his plans." She would teeter through the hall toward her bedroom and wouldn't remember a damn thing the next day.

I'm on edge in this place as it is. I don't want to tempt the wrath of sleepwalking Regina. I put the bag of photo albums at the foot of the bed along with the bowler hat Jack left in my car the last time I saw him.

"Regina," I say softly, stroking the fleshy top of her arm. "Hey, Regina."

Her eyes flash open and she grabs my shoulder tightly. Recognition takes. Regina pulls me to her chest and I'm engulfed in her. She sobs into my neck, holding me tighter, and I have to turn my face so I can breathe. When she lets me go, her face is mottled red and she's laughing. She scrapes away tears from her face with her long, manicured nails.

"I'm sorry," she says. "I haven't seen anybody from back home in so long."

"Nobody's visited? Not Dani?"

"The stripper? Fuck her, excuse my language." Regina dots her eyes with a tissue, checking if her waterproof mascara has held fast. Her lashes still look like thick spider legs. "I haven't heard anything from that one. She knows about it from that little circle of people. You're the only one of his friends I made it a point to call, though. I can't have too many people showing up. It'll overwhelm him."

"What about his dad?" I ask. "Is he coming up from North Carolina?"

Regina pulls her tissue away from her face and her eyes become sharp slits. She moves to the edge of her seat and leans forward. She indicates with a finger that I do the same. "Jack hasn't seen his father since he was a kid," she whispers. "You didn't know that? He never told you that?"

I shake my head.

"I thought he would have told you of all people," Regina says. "He has his reasons, I guess. I won't go into it, but his father lost custodial rights when Jack was four. I'd kill that man if he tried to go anywhere near him."

I could push her for more, but a nurse in white scrubs walks in with Jack alongside her. "The physical therapist said he did great," the nurse says to Regina. They start talking specifics about the therapy. Regina wants to know response times, how his attitude was, question after question. I lose track of their conversation.

The guy in front of me isn't the Jack I was seeing last year. He's Jack at seventeen. His skin is smooth and his face is relaxed. The belly is gone. He's lost at least thirty pounds. This is the Jack who saw someone he knew from my table at the Broadway Diner junior year, sat down next to me when he joined us and started pouring sugar packets on my phone.

Jack's glassy eyes sweep around the room slowly and his bottom lip hangs down. He unlatches the clip of his blue, foam helmet and tosses it under the netted canopy and onto the bed. Regina told me on the phone that the doctors had to chip away at his skull so the swelling wouldn't kill him after the fall. The sight throws me, though. His shaved head is sunken in on both sides of the bone mohawk the doctors cut into him.

I grind my teeth. My Adam's apple feels like it's slicing through all the cords in my throat.

"You remember Annie don't you, Jack?" Regina puts one hand on my back and one on his and pushes us toward each other.

"Okay," Jack says.

I'm not sure he knows me, but he seems to realize he should. He opens his arms and lets me move in for the hug. He's done with it before I am. Jack stretches out on the bed and folds his hands on top of his chest. He remembers something and lifts up his shirt to point to a bandage on his stomach. He starts talking in this garbled language, though his words seem to make sense to him.

"He's trying to tell you about his feeding tube. They had to put the tube in when they induced the coma," Regina says. "He's upset about the scar. This is the big concern in our lives right now." She winks at me.

Jack forgets what he was trying to say or gets bored with us. He puts his hands behind his head and looks up at the canopy netting.

"Jack, I brought a bunch of photos. Do you want to see?" I've been trying to unload one of the sets of prom photos on him for years. He wore a plaid suit to one prom and some purple pimp thing to the other. He owes me.

"Nope," he says.

"That word he knows," Regina tells me. "Don't take it personally. I think it's a good sign. The other day he called this one pain-in-the-ass nurse a bitch, and I thought to myself, 'He's coming back to me.'"

Regina opens up a wheelchair that had been folded against the wall. "It's beautiful out. Let's go sit on the patio." Jack stands and straps his helmet but walks past Regina and the wheelchair. "You know the rules. If you want to go outside, you've got to stay in the chair."

He purses his lips and spits out a stream of random syllables.

"The chair," Regina says, pointing. Jack shrugs and follows her directive. "He knows he won't have to sit in the chair when we finally leave, so he thinks if he can get to go outside without it he'll be allowed to go home. He's tired of this place. Right, Jack?"

He nods without enthusiasm, staring blankly ahead. When we get to the fifth-floor patio, Regina leaves me alone with Jack to buy snacks from a vending machine.

The steam coming off the Schuylkill River makes a swamp of Philadelphia during the summer. The sky is gray and heavy and the whole city feels like it's wrapped in a damp towel. This new Jack doesn't complain about the heat, though I can't say I mind. The old one would have made today miserable for everyone around him just to get the stink of it off of him.

Jack sits slumped in his chair. His skin flushes from the heat and sweat runs down his face from under the helmet. He won't brush it off. He just stares at the concrete building across the street. I'm not sure he's really seeing anything. When a bead of sweat falls into his eyes, he blinks a couple of times, but his hands don't move. This isn't Jack. This isn't even a human anymore. It's just an empty body. Regina's kidding herself.

"You must get pretty bored," I say.

He turns to me. Sounds come out of his throat and his hands gesture as if he's engaged in articulate conversation. It's just mimicry, though. I nod and smile but I can't fake comprehension of whatever this is. He stops talking and returns to his view of the concrete.

Regina returns and gives bottled water to Jack. "Hold it with both hands," she says. Regina looks terrible. I didn't notice it in Jack's dark hospital room, but even in the meager daylight it seems obvious. She always had a round, full face but now she's jowly, as if her skin was yanked down. There are purple tufts of skin under her eyes.

"Has the union been taking care of everything?"

"Damn right, they are. I've got a lawyer on call in case they get cute. There were two other guys got injured on that work site before Jack." She fans her t-shirt against her chest. "It's humid, isn't it? I didn't realize. You can tell how much I get out these days."

Jack starts wailing out of nowhere, this dying bloodhound sort of howl. Regina rubs his arm as she unlocks the wheelchair. "Quiet, baby, please. You're okay. You're okay." She pushes him through the automatic door leading back inside the hospital. When the doors close behind us and we get the full blast of air conditioning, Jack's screams stop. His face is calm and vacant again.

"He does that sometimes," Regina says. "He's not in any pain. He doesn't know a better way to get his point across yet. We're getting there."

Jack takes off his helmet as soon as we're back in his room. When his mother locks the chair, he opens the Velcro on his shoes and takes them off. He kicks his legs under the covers and turns on his side.

"You want to sleep, bud? You want me to leave?" I pat the sheet where his foot should be.

"Yep," he says. He stretches his arms and lets out a monster yawn.

I lift my bag of prom photos. I could leave the duplicates with Regina, but I could also kick her in the shins—it would amount to the same thing. I toss the hat onto Jack's chest. He giggles and holds it out in front of him for inspection.

"You remember that?"

"Ha, bowler derby," he says.

Regina raises her eyebrows, impressed. Jack fits the hat at an angle so it covers a sunken side. I can see the naked part of the scalp throbbing with his pulse.

"One or the other, but yeah," I say. "I've worn it a few times, but it looks better on you."

"Nope," he says. "No, no, no." He sits up and holds the hat out toward me. He thrusts his hand forward with each urgent "no." There's a sharpness to his eyes—the pupils shrink and the muscles in his forehead and temple tense. He's in there, hidden behind those eyes. As soon as I take the cap in my hands, the look is gone. He lies back down on the bed and waves mechanically at me as I walk across the room to leave.

I haven't seen the inside of Finnegan's Wake in two years. Jack had dragged me out my dorm room and into Philadelphia for my twenty-first birthday. It was the only bar he would agree to go to on the rare visits he paid me at college. He hated the place, the other students, my friends—it brought out all his resentments. And he wouldn't hang out in my room or play video games in the student lounge while I was in class. He'd strut around in an army t-shirt and his dad's flak jacket and wait for the children of hippies to pass by and pick arguments with him. He'd stand in front of them and just smile and blow his smoke, waiting for something to happen, disappointed that nothing ever did. It's not like he even believed in the war—he just got a charge out of ruining somebody's moment.

It was better to get him on a train for the twenty-minute ride into Philly. Finnegan's was an easy favorite: the doormen didn't stare too long at your fake license and the bartenders had heavy thumbs.

I've never seen the place in daylight, but they keep the windows boarded up with green planks so it's not like it makes a difference. The same brick-face walls, the same dark wooden tables coated in resin, the same bad lighting. Finnegan's never changes. I pull out a cigarette and the bartender knocks on the counter at the other end of the bar to get my attention. He points to a no-smoking sign, ordinance language in small print underneath, taped to the mirror.

"Philadelphia?" I say. "They got to you too."

The bartender pours my order in front of me, lets me see the two fingers worth of vodka before he adds the ice and the orange juice. The hands are what I notice first. The skin is smooth and his nails are trim and clean. He's a beefy guy, shaved head with a couple days growth and freckles across his nose. He's younger than the bartenders I'm used to, but I've been drinking in the Bayshore too long. I've been walking in old men's worlds. The only people I've spent time with who are my age are beyond repair. This bartender could be anybody. All I need is somebody young and simple to be nice to me, and I'll make myself pathetic for him.

The bartender's walking away, and already I'm slurping the bottom of my drink through the mixer straw to try to get him back here. I'm unlucky, though. He's left the bar to help the waitress unload her lunch orders and the barbacks bring the twenty-pound bags of ice from the back. He carries a bag on each shoulder, slips them into the ice box, and guts the plastic.

I always liked the smallness of Jack's body. There was power hidden in that compact piece of machinery. We would stand with each other in front of a mirror, and if he stepped behind me I couldn't see the top of his head behind mine. With his palm against mine, I could bend my fingers and touch the tips of his. I called them "fag hands," and he would pin my arms above my head with one of those small, strong hands and tickle me hard, digging his stubby fingers into my belly and under my ribcage.

I couldn't do any real damage to him, even when he was asking me to, but the illusion that I could harm him turned me on. There's nothing in this world I want to control now. There's nothing worth controlling. Jack used to say everyone is really a submissive, but some people are too shy to ask for it. I didn't see it then, but I do now. I want to give this fear over to somebody else and let him decide how to give it back to me. The bartender is just a wall of flesh. I could teach him how to make the world small around me.

This day isn't going to end any time soon, but I figure I've got vacation time coming to me or at least comp days. I've had a year of sixty-hour-plus weeks on a $22,000 salary, and nobody's paid me overtime. I'm owed something. I call up my editor, Gill.

"How is your friend?" he says.

"I waited until afternoon to start drinking, so maybe I'm an optimist," I say. "I'm going to need some time off, if that's all right."

"You take a few days. Get your head together," he says. "I'll clear the bureaucracy on this end."

I should thank him, but the bartender sees me shaking my glass and walks back to my end of the bar. All I can do is grunt something before I hang up. The bartender takes away the old glass and slides me another.

"I don't usually do this," I lie. I lower my head, feign penitence. He looks slow enough, maybe he'll believe me. "I was visiting somebody at that brain injury hospital. It's totally fucked."

The bartender nods. "Where was he? Iraq or Afghanistan?"

That's right. That's what Jack's story will be if he ever gets anywhere near normal. He'll break out fake ribbons, buy a uniform on eBay. Nobody will think to question those scars. And I can get him started. "Iraq," I say. "IED."

The bartender hands me a menu. "Why don't you eat something?" he says. "Pick out an appetizer. No charge."

I wave him off. I was wrong. He's too goddamn gentle to be any use for me right now. Put some hours and a few more drinks between us, and I'll imagine him into anything else.

A bachelorette party and a group of UPenn grad students come in one after the other and snatch up all the tables on the first floor. I get very conscious of the fact that I'm the only one drinking alone here. The grad students pound their fists on a table with a weak leg—it rattles endlessly—and bellow, "Guinness." The girls wave their green plastic tiaras and sing some Beyoncé bit. They're killing my Elvis Costello.

I want somebody here with me. Anybody. They don't have to be a friend. They don't even have to like me. On my phone, my contacts from work are mixed in with my life. I can't tell the difference. I text anyone who looks like they might have been from college: *meet me at finnegans.*

I play with my phone, waiting, and listen to the bachelorettes tease my bartender. They're pretty but sloppy, all spackle make-up and glitter. He should know better, but so should I. When someone finally reaches out, it's the wrong person. This kid Mike was a year behind me and used to follow me around when he wasn't stalking anybody else. He must be dry because he keeps texting and when I don't respond, he calls.

"Any other night I'd be there, but our building has the party this weekend," Mike says. "You should come hang out."

It's tempting. The bachelorettes have pulled my bartender down onto a seat at their table and crowned him with a tiara. The bride straddles him and writes on a label on his chest with a magic marker. I tell Mike maybe I'll be there. My glass is empty again and I wave it out in front of me like a beacon, hoping the bartender will see. He uses it as an excuse to detach from the bride. When he finishes my refill, I lean over the counter and stretch the bartender's shirt straight so I can read the sticker the girls gave him. The letters are too curly, and they're moving too fast, but I hold the man still until I can figure them out. The sticker reads, "I am not my penis."

"Those are some dumb bitches," I say.

The girls call, "Calvin, Calvin," across the room. It's a waste, giving him his name like that. I was ready to go the whole night not knowing who he was. He lines up the girls' cosmopolitans on a tray and starts to lift it when I grab his shirt sleeve. He can't leave me right now—let them come and pick up their own drinks.

"My friend used to make fun of retards. He'd do this retard voice and make his hand go limp and slap it on his chest," I say. "Karma got even with him."

There's a pause, a flinch, maybe nothing, but it's there and I've lost the bartender. He's sailing back to the bridesmaids. They're a less pitiful lot.

◊

I'm very careful when I drive drunk. I try to keep under thirty miles per hour, if I can get away with it. The slow-crawl isn't very easy to pull off in Jersey. You look pretty damn conspicuous hunched over the steering wheel, driving ten miles under the limit at night on an empty street when any solid citizen would be speeding. I always made it a point to only drive drunk in towns where I had enough connections to squeeze out of a traffic stop. As long as I didn't harm life or property, I figured I could count on getting a ride home and the mess of the night cleared from any docket or police blotter. It never came to that because, like I said, I'm careful.

In Philly, I avoid the main thoroughfares and stick to the one-lane, one-way streets where you have to stop at every intersection. The Philadelphia side streets are tight, with cars parked on either side of the driving lane. You would have enough cause to go fifteen or twenty miles per hour sober.

I'm heavy on the break and jerk to a stop whenever I see a flash of red anywhere. Every couple of blocks I get some asshole riding my fender and I have to turn my front end into whatever empty spot of concrete I can manage. Backing out of that crooked parking job is when I panic. Reverse seems a reasonable gear most of the time, but the scene in my rearview is something I can't make sense of. I open my door and plant a foot on the ground, only reversing as fast as my foot can step backward as I watch for the cars parked behind me. It seems too complicated, more than it should be, but I manage.

I arrive at the dorm to find Mike wearing a tuxedo jacket, a purple cummerbund, and tropical print boxer shorts. The outfit is typical party-wear for Mike, but he's short and skeletal and has to keep adjusting the pieces so they don't fall out of place. He hasn't changed since I saw him last year. His skin is still pale and his eyes bug out behind his glasses like an ugly Chihuahua.

Mike goes in for the hug. I don't like anybody touching me, but especially Mike. He's an awkward hugger, holding onto you for too long while he digs his pointy chin into your shoulder and rubs his hands up and down your back. All his girlfriends luck into the treatment.

I've forgotten why we became friends. Probably loneliness, and then I didn't know any better, and loneliness turned into loyalty. Neither seems a worthwhile reason anymore, but I can't figure how to change things or if it would be worth the effort.

He's been talking about the new job he's starting in the fall. I'm not listening. The liquor isn't in the kitchen or the common room. Maybe the basement? Maybe a different apartment? Mike leans in too close and his sour breath bears down on me.

"I know what you're thinking: How does a physics major become a financial risk consultant," he says.

"Constantly," I say. "I'm going to wander."

I claim an air mattress in an apartment on the second floor where the foot traffic seems to be moving. A couple of chemistry majors are walking around from apartment to apartment with a hand towel and a container of ether they stole from the lab. They regulate the goods, not letting the bottle get out of sight. They use a cloth to cover the bottle, and their noses and mouths, then they breathe in the fumes and giggle like electric clowns. When the ether reaches me, I hold it up to eye level and swirl the liquid around, not that I can see much through the amber glass. A chemistry major rushes across the room with his hands in front of his chest.

"Relax. I won't spill it," I say. "What does it do for you?"

"You get drunk without the hangover," the chemistry major says. The laugh tracks are still high-pitched and whirring around me. I don't believe him, but it's not like I'm particular. I bring the bottle to my nose and cover my face.

The ether ices over my nasal passages and throat. I open my eyes and they start tearing. The cold reaches my chest, and I'm apart from the surface of things. Somebody takes the cloth and the bottle. I put the heels of my palms against my eyelids and push deeply into my eye sockets until I get the black I'm seeing to change to orange.

The pain starts in my temples and pushes up through my teeth. I have to think about my breath, force it up through a tight throat, and my pulse slows. Everybody here is looking after their own disappearing act. I start gurgling and laughing like the other bored morons. Whatever control I had over myself is over. The high is over. I could go for another round but the ether and the chemistry majors are gone.

There are two girls facing each other on the futon. The Asian alterna-chick is letting the chubby redhead run her fingers along her arms in a slow rhythm, off-time from the dance music. Their eyes are closed and the alterna-chick turns her head toward the ceiling, her lips moving but barely. I want to ask them what they're on, but I'm drowsy from the down-swing of the ether. The nausea breaks and my face is slick and cold.

Mike sits beside me and talks to the side of my face. He hasn't said anything interesting in four years, so I keep watching the girls.

"Can I?" he says. When I don't answer, he opens a couple buttons on my blouse and puts his hand inside. He cups my bra but then doesn't move, until eventually he slips his hand under the cloth. When I left Finnegan's, I expected the night would go here. I was ready to let it happen and hate myself for it later. He pinches my nipple between his thumb and forefinger and tugs it forward and back. This awkward mess, I wasn't expecting. I think Mike is milking me.

He leans in to kiss my neck and I fall onto my side laughing. I wrap both my hands around his wrist and bring his palm up to my mouth so he can feel it. He struggles against me, but I just twist his arm tighter.

"Let go of me, you stupid bitch," Mike says. He braces his foot against my hip and kicks himself free.

Newsletter to 4,000 Subscribers

Stephen Elliott

The Part About the Sun Setting on the Ocean

I'm trying to write about this woman I love, but maybe too much has been written about her, the way too much has been written about Las Vegas. Last night we were eating dinner. She was wearing jeans, and I had my hand on the inside of her thigh, and she asked how long I was going to wait. I don't think I answered. I know better than to take the bait. Later I mentioned I had written something about her. I didn't mention that it was coming out in an anthology. She asked me to read it at the performance later. In the essay I talk about rejection as foreplay. I say I love her but I don't like her.

A few hours before the reading I taught a writing class—the reason they brought me out here. Before that, I stood in the pool with a performance artist, our arms raised above our heads, talking about a child.

The stage is always glamorous. It's why students fall in love with teachers. But the paint starts to peel the moment the performance is over and you go back to being like everybody else, or worse.

At the end of the night, I was outside the casino in the dark. It was still hot and dry, only a shade more bearable than the daytime. I thought about Eli, who has a theory. His theory is that with most people, when you meet them, they seem well-put-together, and as you get to know them you find that they're actually all kinds of screwed up, and, as you get to know them more, you find that underneath that is a third layer of bedrock, where they're actually pretty solid. He once told me that I was the reverse—that at first I seemed like a mess, but as he got to know me I seemed really solid, but beneath that I was truly a mess. I had a foundation in sand.

Who's to say?

The point is she had asked how long I would wait, and at night I started to think how easy it was to love her. It was perfectly safe, like loving a streetcar you saw pass by once. She said, "You're never going to quit, are you?" And I thought, *There is no end game here.*

◇

Which Part of Yourself Did You Bring to the Party

I was thinking about the *New York Times*, and how I'd never been reviewed in their weekday section, how only one of my seven books had ever gotten a full review in the Sunday book review, and two others with brief mentions.

Last night I met a woman wearing red. She wanted to talk about her book, a lot. She was obsessed with agents and proposals and what she had been told in a workshop and at a retreat. I said, "Stop." I said, "The reason no one will publish your book is that you haven't written it." She told me her story, which was interesting enough, but everybody has an interesting story; it's only the language that will make it worth reading. She said she knew. She would focus on the writing. But then she had four kids, and how did I support myself? I said she couldn't get by on what I make. She asked what I was working on and I said I wrote emails. I'd been trying to return to another conversation, a few feet away, with a friend, one of my favorite people in the entire world. He was drunk (or maybe just a little buzzed) and he's overly friendly when he's been drinking. He had wrapped his arm around my neck and I felt like a well-looked-after younger brother. I wanted to get back to that. She brought up her book proposal again, and what she'd been told. I gave her my full attention. I thought, *It's hard to be good sometimes.* I said, "You have to stop." I said nothing she was saying had anything to do with writing a book. And she agreed, but then started over. She has so many children, she popped them out like gumballs. Her first husband had passed away. We were on the second floor of a mansion. The walls were painted mustard. I thought I would like to paint my walls that color. Her skin was incredible, as if she was pregnant again.

She practically glowed in that way pregnant women glow sometimes (I shouldn't talk about pregnant women; I don't know anything about them, but sometimes it seems like their skin gets very nice). Earlier, I'd had a conversation with the homeowner about group-home kids and scholarship children and how the main difference was that kids from poor homes didn't get second chances. It's not enough to give a child one chance. What kind of child will make it, given only one chance? The ability to survive a fall is the definition of privilege. I put my hands on her shoulders and looked straight at her. I said she had to let it go. Anyone could see she was driving herself crazy. It was like watching someone walk into a fire.

In another situation I would say, "Lady, that building is burning and you won't be able to save anything. You'll die from smoke inhalation before the first flame catches your skirt."

Before that it was raining a little and I bicycled up 17th Street, over the hill. I was breathing heavy. It was early in the evening and the sky was as gray as primer. There were people walking dogs and a house with iron work surrounding the third floor. I love when San Francisco is like this—when the rain becomes the air and it feels like you're in a movie. The weather was changing as I descended toward the base of Twin Peaks and then up, away from the university. I was thinking about somebody I couldn't see, about a body bag and a hood, imagining being left like that for an hour and a half. I stopped at the beginning of the block. I'd had a conversation that morning with a woman I was in love with. She said I was a slut. She wanted to know the other woman's name, the one with the body bag, but I wouldn't tell her. We talked about doing photo shoots in my new studio. I said that was fine. I said we could do audio recordings if she wanted. I was making a joke. It would take time, and I was thinking about someone else. The person I was thinking about wore leather shorts and a corset and had long black hair and boots and we were in a basement and there were curtains everywhere and chains and other pieces of equipment hanging from the wall. She was looking for something and someone I'd never seen before came in to help her find it. It was memory. It was wet out and I was filled with desire as I ascended the stairs and a man in a long apron and a tie said he didn't think I'd need to lock my bike. I slid the U-lock through the tire and the frame anyway, before going inside.

◇

That's Why They Call It New York

After the reading I went to the Fleshbot Awards (NSFW). There were several worlds colliding there. Jonathan Ames was presenting and the editors of all the large blogs were in attendance. Of course, there were tons of sex workers. And there were sex workers who were also artists and there were sex workers who were just sex workers. I won't go into detail, but lets say I knew more people than I thought I would. There was a woman there who represented stability, and another who represented chaos, and also a third woman who was nice but represented neither chaos nor stability. We would just become friends.

At one point, I ended up on my knees behind the woman that represented chaos, blood pouring from my nose, my hand inside her long, black skirt while she typed into her cell phone a quick blog post about how this wasn't really working for her. And the woman that represented stability, who was also a friend, was standing nearby, leaning against the railing, and our eyes met for a second, and I thought I would never go on a date with that woman now. To my left was the photo gallery with the large light setup and stripper poles. Later, Ames and I ended up on either side of the third woman. I don't remember what we were talking about, but it was nice because they were both nice. We weren't in a hurry. It was already one in the morning. A drink had been spilled, and the couch was soaked, so we sat close together to avoid the mess.

Of course, this doesn't tell you much about book tours, but it does say something about New York and the kind of parties you can get into, even wearing gym shoes. And also about the link between sex workers, bloggers, and old media types as well as the people writing and acting in television shows, and people who think of themselves as literary writers, and why New York has nothing in common with the rest of the country except that every small town has lost a few to Gotham City.

I Wish I Wish

I was thinking this morning, while listening to the *Harold and Maude* soundtrack, how far are we away from a world divided between people who live online and people who don't? I think you know what I mean. Not that people online don't meet for drinks or go out to eat. But there will be a split where the Internet is no longer a phenomenon—it just is. And there will be people communicating online, and there will be people who aren't into it. We have this belief that everything is going online, but that's going to stop at some point, like a neighborhood that was gentrifying just before the bubble burst, and so the Google employees learn to live with the artists and the immigrants, and nobody really talks about why there's a dollar store on one block and a hamburger costs $13 on the next.

"Don't you have an iPhone?" someone asked me yesterday. I said I did— it was my laptop. It's just an older version, and it's a little big and clunky, but still works OK.

Subway Judge

Lisa Badner

Two peed,
but called it passing water.
One spat, one smoked,
fourteen couldn't swipe.
Nine doubled-up,
four crawled under, six jumped over.
Seven walked between cars: two were faint,
three smelled a homeless person,
one had diabetes and one had gout.
Two wheelchairs, two walkers, six strollers,
four high wheels, six gates. One chased by a rapist.
One fake snake.
Four cried. Three for real.
One sleeper, two leaners, three feet, six bags.
Eight tourists. Two suits.
Eleven on welfare. One Croatian.
One Jew. I was caught snacking three times,
under my desk. I was
twice admonished through glass,
to use "system," "tender," "fare media,"
to wear my badge.
My phone vibrated once.
I was told four times,
turn it off.

Computer Eighties

from The Eighties, a Brief Primer

Michael Reid Busk

Computers were invented in the Eighties. The earliest versions were analog computation devices constructed from giant tubes—at the very start, elaborate McDonald's playhouses. Computer scientists would fill the playhouses with children, each of whom carried a different number of note cards, and that number was also written in neon green on both the fronts and backs of their oversized t-shirts. If you wanted to know the sum of three and five, you sent a child scout with three index cards in his or her pocket into the massive, multi-story labyrinth. Other children marked with numerals crowded the tubes, waiting with a Christmas Eve eagerness for the scout, who climbed and crawled and slid through the ducts, over and under and around the other children, calling out for the five. A desperate four or six might stop the scout, saying they were close enough, but the scout would scowl them down, telling them no, this was mathematics, this was the future. When the scout finally found the five, they would wiggle and scoot through the intestinal tubing until they found the exit, where a computer scientist in a lab coat would be waiting for them to count their cards and say that the sum was indeed eight, as predicted.

Gradually, computing became more efficient, more powerful. Milestones included: punch cards, Pong, the brief craze of jewelry constructed from the perforated margins of dot matrix paper, and nuclear war simulators which sometimes had to be cajoled into not destroying the world.

But computers could do more than tell you how many angels could dance on the head of a pin, more than beat you badly at chess (see *Russian Eighties*). Computers made it possible to communicate almost instantaneously. Through a dial-up modem, anyone could post messages on the various BBSs (bulletin board systems) that were springing up everywhere, and hundreds of people would immediately reply: *Where's the beef?* Or: *I'm not a serial killer, but I play one on TV.* Or: *Obsession? Don't mind if I do.* Or: *Quarter Pounder, half nelson, single malt, Double*

Jeopardy, triple axel (see *Brian Boitano Eighties*). Or: *Sometimes I just wish I could get a lobotomy, believe in God, and be happy.* Before computers, people communicated through the post, or face-to-face, or by carrier pigeon, but most commonly, through singing telegrams. It was cheery, strolling down residential streets and hearing red-suited young men (usually former McDonald's playhouse scouts) ask a family in perky melody if they would like to come over to the Johnsons and watch *Dallas.*

As computers improved, the Johnsons and others families would instead post such invitations on BBSs, to which their neighbors could reply as wittily and immediately as they liked. But streets grew sullenly quiet, and the jobless telegram boys, formerly the happiest of professionals, became brooding, vengeful Luddites. They had been right: computers were the future, and in their late teens, they were already the past. Many refused other forms of work, demanding reparations for their grievances. Some wandered towns in droves, wishing their parents were still proud of them. Finally they came to despise all technology, setting fire to cars, making shelters in the forested curls of golf courses, throwing rocks at robots. Too poor for anything else, they would storm their local McDonald's restaurants at off-peak hours, ordering heavy sacks of food, demanding free refills and extra cheese. Adjusting their fraying bowties, wiping Big Mac sauce from their lips, they spoke glowingly of pre-industrial life, minstrels and square dances and the abacus. They used four-letter words when discussing Henry Ford and Alan Turing, grieved that men didn't wear bowties anymore.

With stomachs full and hearts unburdened but for bile, they would sometimes race each other through the playhouses, despite surpassing the areas' forty-eight inch maximum height restrictions. Now and again one of them would wriggle over a small note card stuck between seams in the bright molded plastic. Pulling it out, he'd read the number, tracing his finger over what might have been an eight and might have been infinity. Tucking it into the inner pocket of his threadbare red velvet jacket, he would call out to his comrades, his voice echoing off the tubes: *Between love and madness lies obsession.*

In the Early Morning Cypress Grove

Michael Schiavo

The man has announced we cannot go on

    no longer like we do. Say goodbye to the bells I

        waiting in the station long time for your call.

    President Lincoln freed the slaves

in less time it takes you tell me how/how not.

    How warped these carnation rays to the fairly

        full moon misting to once I remember black

    your hair 'round the cloud-tipped spires of your mind

when I look down at my heart.

    It all topples in a bucket of blueberries too sweet

        much too for pie. You might have to stare

    long distance past the mountains rising up

'round my valley to ever find me again. That gone

    goodbye but what delirious elm shall I do?

        Without you the world's the same sad strum.

    You imagine the orchestra wild but here

a man who can without you barely hold a tune.

    Good on the kazoo. For which you will not

        return never who would? Was a land some time

    hard in brown & green. All the things you said

to me I wish I could recite. Dark eyes.

    What little distance enormous between us.

Winter in the air still fall. Unendingly here

this inescapable & the last to admit

how I must've seemed through the whole

carnival 'til we got to the riverbank. Fireside.

I draw a circle around me only you can enter.

Those days in bed we never had talking

Philip Guston fireflies loving cake hotness

the war what it means to find in another

yourself but brighter & alive.

Now only winter. Nothing until buds

on the white trees whiten my forgetfulness.

Every tongue on earth will speak your name

from now until the overture is buried

they singing Jairan to the end of it or near

the end. Nothing as you know ever really

only that the Allegheny becomes the Ohio.

All the questions then after

the horoscopes I can see you still from the corner

in the corner of my heart doing all. Over

over in the most perfect gauze of darkness.

Bells are ringing somewhere in the city you live.

Metaphor

Peter Harris

I couldn't put down the book about my kind
of cancer. It appealed to my love of metaphor:
the visitor starts as a mild-mannered gentleman,
who shapeshifts into a percolator, a steamroller,
a force that erodes and sucks breathtakingly.

The prostate: a walnut, a dwarf lemon,
a miniature Grand Central Station
with a Lincoln Tunnel inside that you pee through.
It's tucked away like the Lost Ark,

booby trapped, much as this book is spiked
with frightening scores, pictures, facts.
But it's fun imagining
a five-boroughed crab apple, a cave
full of grapes, a gift box
that sometimes secretes poison chocolates,

the same box I'm toting as I try to cross
a spring river. It's flooding and I'm jumping
from ice floe to ice floe, each a metaphor,
a moment's release from time and decay.

Yes, I am crossing the spring river. If I can
string together enough jumps, I'll make it
to the far shore. A shore, I hope,
a solid fact, not just another metaphor.

The Crossing

Ann Robinson

The air blackens and someone whispers
The devil is among us. The fans shut on and off
in the transport truck

and walls strain with heat. The tropic pulse
is not of the body but the clay earth that brought us here.

Nothing is imagined. Not the sound
of an engine being stalled or boots on gravel.

The yellow eyes of the border patrol as the door slides open.
We have decided what to do
and run out into the August stars. Guns fire off.

I duck into the landscape,
become the tallest of trees, moon along the sides,
look down, the small lives along the road,

A man cradles what's left of him, a woman simply folds.
The only sound was a long time ago.

I almost cannot believe. A child tries to fly
among these leaves.

Bunnyman

Matthew S. Baker

His father pointed with a bloody finger. "Here. Right here, between the stomach and the liver."

Jacob knelt on the ground of the forest, on dry, hard-packed snow with the dead rabbit he had shot lying peeled open between him and his father. It steamed. His hands, shaking from the thrill of the hunt, lay on his twenty-two. They were numb from the morning cold. He wanted to put them in the warmth of the rabbit.

"Where?" He shook his head. Jacob had watched his father do this thing—quickly, quietly, delicately field dress a rabbit—but had never done it himself or learned how. "Not till your fingers are nimble enough," his father always told him. Finally, they were nimble.

With all ten of his own fingers, his father pushed apart the purple sacs inside the rabbit, which no longer looked like a rabbit, and a black acorn-sized thing emerged. His father nodded at it, his hands full of organ. "There. Now do you see it?"

Now he did.

His father picked up from the snowy ground the knife he had used to cut off the rabbit's head, slice open its side, and skin it. He flicked his wrist twice and the black thing was stuck on the tip of the knife, and the knife was pointed right at Jacob's nose. "Lookit," his father said. "It's the vestigius."

He looked at it. It shone green, and then red, and then black again. The blood glistened in the early gray light that pushed through the thin cloud cover and the trees overhead. A breeze rattled the leaves still dangling precariously from their limbs. From behind him came the sound of a snapped twig. He twisted quickly and thought, *The Bunnyman*, and his father looked up, but there was nothing there. They waited, did not speak. Still, nothing. He turned back to his father, who shook the knife at him again.

"This is junk," his father said. "Toss it out, never eat it."

"OK."

"Most times, the vestigius is nothing, harmless, but sometimes, when the rabbit's too old and blind to pick out the good food from the bad, his insides turn rotten. You can't tell by looking, though. You don't know what's good and what's rotten on the inside. A good vestigius looks just like a bad one."

"OK."

"Swear." He jabbed the thing-tipped knife at Jacob. "You'll never eat it. Dig around it, cut it out, throw it away. Find something else to eat instead of rabbit if you're not sure you can find it on your own. It's better to go for squirrel than risk eating a bad vestigius."

Jacob crossed his chest. His hands were done shaking, but they were still cold. "I swear."

"Can you find it on your own?"

"Yessir."

"Good boy. To home."

Several times as they walked, Jacob thought he heard something behind them. From the way his father took his hand, pulled him close, and walked a touch quicker, he knew his father heard something too.

The third time he heard a noise—a bristling too tentative to be the wind—his father gave his hand a squeeze. "If anything should happen to me," he said, "you go right to Mr. Marks, hear?"

"Why?" Jacob asked. His father hated Mr. Marks. Few things were clearer to Jacob than that.

"He'll take care of you."

"He hates me."

"He hates *me*. But he'll take care of you."

"Why?"

His father did not answer, but Jacob did not press. After all, it would be a busy day—once finished dressing the rabbit back at the cabin, they had to get to town and back before dark—and talking slowed them down. And these days the winter sun fell quickly, and the dark time afterwards was a time of fear and uncertainty.

◊

Home was a cabin, old but sturdy and well sealed. Jacob was proud of it.

He never wanted to leave. His great-grandfather built it ages ago, before the railroad came, when the Bunnyman was still only a legend. Back then, it was isolated. An hour in all directions until you reached any real road, and another hour on the road until you reached a town. By the time Jacob was old enough to wander the woods by himself—but only in the daytime, of course, only when he could see the things that might chase him—it was no more than half that. His father said it wouldn't be long before the towns were right on top of them and they awoke each morning to smells of stale garbage and piss rather than the sweet scent of pine.

Now as they approached their cabin, the light of the sun found a hole in the clouds and glittered the crusted snow that still lay largely unbroken around most of the small one-room home, save the path Jacob and his father had forged between the door and the outhouse around the back.

He set the sack of rabbit bits on the red-stained stump where his father cleaned the bigger kills, then retrieved from inside the salt tin. For half an hour, Jacob and his father pressed salt against the rabbit's muscles to turn them into meat. The clearing around them was frozen and still and quiet; then, in the distance, a train whistle, the scream of steel and oil.

"I ain't leaving," his father mumbled. "They push on us, we'll push right back." He said this, or something like it, whenever the whistle blew.

"Yep," Jacob said. "We will."

Jacob agreed with his father, in this and in everything else, because he was still a child—not even a whole person, just an extension of his father. He only ever thought as his father thought and did as his father did, trusting always, doubting never.

They went to town. Jacob carried over his shoulder a slew of rabbit pelts ready to be sold. His father went into the leather store to sell the pelts to Mr. Marks. Jacob waited outside, as his father told him to do—so he would not hear the two men shout. It was unclear what they shouted about, but Jacob did not want to hear it. It was an adult argument, and anyway, other children sat outside as well, on stacks of lumber and nail crates, and they had their own arguments, more relevant arguments. About the Bunnyman.

He lives by the bridge, they whispered to each other. In the woods. The new railroad bridge over the main road into town. He hangs kids from its braces. Flays them. Tans their hides. Wears them as boots and mittens. He came on the railroad from the east—no, the north—no, the far, far south. He is a shadow, only visible in the brightness of day, and only in the open—in the woods, where the trees keep out the sun, he walks, pads, prowls unseen. He slashed that woman in the woods, just last year he did.

Jacob added nothing to the conversation, though he knew things the others did not. Or, more precisely, he knew the Bunnyman more precisely. The Bunnyman was tall, like a man, and covered in fur. His ears were not the ears of rabbits, but they were longer than a person's, and high on his head. The moonlight danced and shivered when he was near, never touched him—it left a shadow in the shape of him, a silhouette that left him sharply defined, against the lighted woods and in the mind, but without details. He was a thing you saw by not seeing it. And he knew that the Bunnyman's claws were sharp and strong from the grooves they left in the snow and from the ease with which they sliced his mother open the July before on her way home from town. From her throat to her bellybutton, a narrow line of blood through the slit in her clothes for an instant, then a river of it overflowing, soaking into her dress and the warm summer soil. The sacks of flour and cornmeal and the jar of ammonia spilled from the crate she carried. She was too terrified to scream. It hurt badly, but she had fought; her fingertips had fur on them, stuck with blood too black to be her own. He whispered in her ear, "Tell me where your family lives," but she was silent, despite the agony of her wounds. But no, it did not hurt at all. She went peacefully, immediately, she never saw it coming. The Bunnyman had surprised her, come from behind a tree. The crate she carried was stacked high and had blocked her view of him, and so suddenly, she was dead. It was like falling asleep in the midday sun, when the heat clings to your eyelids, drags them down and down, and fighting it is impossible.

But really, Jacob knew none of this, not like he knew other things; he was not there when it happened, he had not seen the Bunnyman. He imagined his mother's death both ways and did not try to reconcile them: She died a tortured hero; she died without pain. This is what he knew.

He and his father had searched for her when the three of them should have been eating their supper, but it was July, so it was not yet sundown. They came upon her suddenly, torn open on the forest floor. The fumes from the burst ammonia jar pierced Jacob's nose.

The stories he heard from the other children were wrong, but he liked them. They were like the ones his father used to tell him before bed—pleasantly impossible. The truth—about beans or mirrors or spinning wheels or rabbit-shaped men—was harder to face.

◊

That night, some time after they returned to the cabin with their satchel filled with coins and their arms filled with bundles, it stormed. Wind, snow, fallen trees.

His father stewed some of the rabbit with carrots and turnips. The fresh pelt hung on a hook on the wall. After supper, they would soak it in a salt-and-alum tanner and leave it for two days, and then clean it of its stubborn flesh, and then soak it some more, and then dry it and fluff it and work it soft. He could smell the tanner even more than he could smell the stew, and so his food tasted bitter.

As they ate, he asked his father, "What's a vestigius do?"

"Do?"

"If you eat it. If you don't cut it out."

"It'll kill you. Eventually."

"How will it kill you?"

His father looked at him. "Slowly," I said.

"But how?"

"Hm." The wind blew hard against the cabin. Snow piled up on the muntins in the windows. "Like a poison. Like a knife in your belly."

Jacob stiffened. He remembered his mother, the slice in her belly. The chair she used to sit in at supper had not been touched since she got up from breakfast that morning. He almost touched it now, but he knew the wood would not be warm under his skin.

They sat for a minute.

"Was it really the Bunnyman?" He whispered this.

His father stirred his stew. He wiped at his beard, straightened his collar. "Yes. It was the Bunnyman."

"Why?"

His father shrugged. "Nobody knows."

"I'll kill him right back." Jacob, by now, had forgotten about the bitterness of the air. He was saturated with it and it no longer affected him.

"No. He's worse to you if you hunt him. Nobody hunts the Bunnyman anymore."

"How do you know?"

"I know people. I've heard stories that'd keep you up at night."

"Tell me."

"No."

"How come?"

Outside, a thud. A branch, Jacob thought, fallen.

"They'd keep you up at night."

The storm did not let up. It battered their tiny cabin, tore down birch trees just outside. But Jacob was calm because he could see that his father was calm, and they did not leave the cabin. They ate from their cupboard, and for water they opened the window just enough to scrape a potful of snow from the sill to melt. His father dusted the portrait of his mother that sat on the mantelpiece, and her face shone in the candlelight. In front of a warm stove fire, they read their books: his father had his Bible, which made him laugh as he read it; he had *The Wilderness Survival Manual*, which showed pictures of stick compasses and snares made of saplings.

Two days after they shot the rabbit, it was time to clean the hide. It sat in the bucket of tanner in the corner of the cabin farthest from the beds, covered with a tarpaulin to keep the bitter smell away. Jacob, wearing an apron too large for him, pulled the hide from the tanner with wooden tongs almost as long as he was, and he hung it from a cord strung up above the bucket so the drops of tanner would fall back into it. Then his father used his knife to scrape the fat away from the skin. It came off in one piece. He threw it in the fire. They watched it crackle and burn. The hide was clean now, but not soft enough. They soaked it in more tanner, with more salt and more alum. It would sit for seven days.

They went back to their chairs and their books. Jacob looked up words he had learned on his last trip into town in his manual: *camphor*, from the general store clerk; *flax*, from the manager of the dry-goods store; *cuckold*, from Mr. Marks's argument with his father, which was not listed. He looked up *vestigius*, but learned nothing new. Under *Bunnyman*—the last entry under B, on a well-worn page— "A threatening being once thought to be only legend, since verified with photographic elements." Strangely, there was no photograph there. It continued, "Origin unknown, habitat unknown, diet unknown (although presumed to be similar to that of rabbits. See *rabbit*.)."

He pondered these words, then realized he had private business to do. He told his father, who looked out the window to the outhouse. The storm sounded no different. Hard wind, whistling branchlets, uprooted trees. Snow whorled.

"OK," his father said. "I'll go with you."

They put on their mackinaws and overcoats and rabbit-fur mittens. His father took a shovel from the corner and opened the front door. A snow wall stood there, three feet high, and more snow was falling on top of it. Some blew into the cabin.

Jacob said, "Will the shovel provoke him?"

"No, it shouldn't." His father looked at the shovel. "No," he said again, more quietly. He closed the door again, then took a lantern from the shelf and lit it. "Ready?"

They braced against each other. His father opened the door and pushed into the snow. His father's legs were strong; they plowed the drifts and made a path. His mother used to admire those legs. "See what they can do?" she would say as he lifted fallen trees out of their paths through the woods. "See how they work for him just like they should?"

The wind and the flakes blistered the sliver of Jacob's face that remained open to it. He closed his eyes and followed his father's form, hands on his waist. Jacob wondered, not for the first time, why they had no bucket for this sort of thing in the cabin, where it was warm. They arrived at the outhouse as a train whistle sounded in the distance, somehow making its way through the storm to their ears. His father dug out room for the door to open, and Jacob went in and did his business. He stayed longer than he had to—it was warm inside, and the air was still—but his father banged on the door and shouted something through the wood, so he went outside again.

His father stepped in. "Wait for me," he said, and handed Jacob the shovel.

Wind burned his cheeks, his nostrils. His fingers were numb, even mittened. The train whistled again, the snow kept falling—no, not falling; spinning, rising, pressing in on all sides, with no clear origin. Jacob knew it had to fall to arrive at the ground, but he could not see it fall. He could see nothing but the shine of the lamp in the window of the cabin, where he wanted to be. Everywhere else was black, or white.

A snap. In the woods. Behind him. He turned. He knocked on the door. His father mumbled.

Another crack. A pop. Behind him again, always where he wasn't looking. He called out. No answer, not even from inside the outhouse. He banged on the door. The wind came on loud and hard, and if there was an answer this time, he did not hear it. The light from the window went weak—the snow between him and it was thickening, deepening.

A knock, and a noise—a chirruped howl, a grinding squeal. He held the shovel like an axe. Snow piled at his feet, buried them. He kicked it loose, he could not stop his feet. He danced in the snow, waiting for his father. He banged, but nothing came. No sounds but the echoes in his ears of the noises he did not want to hear.

Jacob ran. Nothing set him off, no new screams or creaks in the distance, just their echoes in his mind. He ran, the best he could in the drifts, across the yard to the door, and in. He stripped himself of his wet clothes, stood by the fire. He watched the snowflakes that had blown in the door. As they warmed, they turned from white to the floor's gray color, from snow to water, and then disappeared into nothing.

The window did not let him see his father. When he was far away, by the fire, the glare from the lantern was all there was. He took down the lantern, but then there was no light outside to see by. He put the lantern back up but stood up against the window to see past the glare. His breath fogged the window, and he could see nothing. With the corner of the blanket, he wiped the window pane clear again. All he saw then was his own face, red at the round places. He shivered in the cold.

For hours, he waited—for the storm to let up, for his father to return. For hours, for days. He thought of a story his father told him once, of a man in a blizzard so thick that he got lost on his way back from using the outhouse, found frozen half a mile from it, half a mile plus ten yards from the cabin. In the meantime, Jacob went in a bucket in the corner, next to the tanner, where it reeked already, anyway.

When the outside finally calmed, Jacob went out to get his father. His legs were not strong; he had to dig a trench around the cabin. When he could see the outhouse he stopped to rest, just looked at it. He called for his father, but heard nothing. Snow was piled high everywhere.

The outhouse looked tiny from this distance, like the doghouses he had seen on the trips into town. There were no tracks, no pits where his father might have dug himself out. After some minutes he went to it, waded through the snow like his father had done, with the shovel held high. It was slow going; his legs were weak, not like his father's at all.

Jacob pounded on the door, at the top of it, and said to his father, "I'm here, Daddy, don't you worry," and then he dug. Mounds of snow grew up behind him and around him, and soon he was surrounded by it, buried himself, and now he was down to the short piece of rope they used as a door handle, and now he was down to the bottom, and now he was pulling open the door, smiling because he found his father.

And, indeed, his father was there, resting quietly on the seat of the outhouse—hands squeezed underneath his arms as if to be warmed, feet straight forward, eyes closed, lips stained with the same purplish blue that blackberry juice left on them those midsummer evenings when they went picking, work done for the day and the sun still high. He wore a sash of blood, a dark stain that followed the same path, from his shoulder to his groin, as the long, jagged slice in his coat.

Jacob closed the door to the outhouse and climbed out of the hole he had dug. His tears, as he walked back to the cabin, were warm on his face, and this is why—he told himself—he did not try to stop them from coming.

He changed his father's coat—put him in something intact, so as to require no explanation—and wiped the blood spatter from his face with a wet cloth, and then he went into town to tell Mr. Marks that his father was dead. From the cold, he said. Not from the Bunnyman, who Jacob was sure was no match for his father. It must have been the cold that slowed him down, made him vulnerable.

Mr. Marks was feeble. That's what Jacob thought. He walked around his store like a stubborn old man, slowly, barely making it from shelf to shelf, but he did not use a cane. He refused one. But he was not that old, and was kindly whenever he saw Jacob, always gave him a piece of penny candy from the jar at the counter. It tasted more of leather than of peppermint or butterscotch, having sat out too long in a room full of animal skins.

On this visit, though, Mr. Marks did not smile. He shuffled his way over to Jacob and offered his condolences. He put his hand on Jacob's shoulder and said, "I suppose you'll be moving in here with me, then." He lived over the store, in what seemed like a small apartment. Jacob only ever saw it from the dusty street outside.

"Why would I?" Jacob said.

Mr. Marks said, "You're a little boy. What else choice do you have? What other relations?"

"Home," Jacob said. "The cabin. In the woods."

"You can't live out there on your own," Mr. Marks said. "You can't possibly take care of yourself."

"What relations?" Jacob said. "You're no relations." Mr. Marks went red and quiet, and Jacob did too. Then, "I live in the cabin in the woods."

"But what about the Bunnyman?"

A pause, and again, quiet. "I live in the cabin in the woods."

"Well. OK then," said Mr. Marks. "I suppose I'll check up on you now and again."

The two of them went back to the cabin with a handful of other men and a wagon and carted his father off to the cemetery to be buried next to his mother. The headstones, even the tall ones, only peeked out over the blinding white. Jacob watched the men work with a careful eye, making sure they did not expose the gash in his father's torso. One of them asked him what faith his father was. He answered how his father always did, said he believes in the goodness of a good meal and a good woman. The man turned to the others and said, "No ceremony."

There was nothing more to do, then, than watch the hole be dug—slowly, slowly, since the snow was thick and the ground was frozen—and he was glad, because next to the place where they buried his father was the blank space reserved for him, and when he saw it he could think of nothing but the Bunnyman slicing open his own belly and tearing out his guts. Not his father, not how terrible a death he had had, sitting there, trapped in a tiny room and inches above frozen shit, while snow piled up around him and penned him in. Not his mother, in her own grave just yards from him now, the quiet woman with the thin, hard lips that hummed him to sleep each night and whose voice still spoke to him when he tensed his body and a thin roar filled his ears, washed out the sounds of the world.

By the time he got back to the cabin, it was dark. He was alone; Mr. Marks said he would come in a week. As he sat over a bowl of canned pears from the cupboard, he was consumed by thoughts of the

Bunnyman like never before. He told himself he would hunt it, track it like his father had taught him to track rabbits, only better, smarter, more warily.

That night, he slept in his father's pajamas and his father's bed, but he panicked when he awoke and the door and the windows were in the wrong places, before he remembered he was not in the same place he used to be. The night after that, he slept in his own bed, but after he awoke—calmly, because he had dreamed of a warm sun—he panicked again, because his father's bed was empty, and his father was dead. He spent the next few nights moving the beds around, trying different combinations of mattress and orientation, and soon became comfortable with any arrangement so long as it was different from the one he used the night before.

◊

It was winter; there was not much to eat, even from the cupboard. He hunted for his food.

In winter, white-tailed deer—animals Jacob had hunted with his father many times before—were scarce. To see one in the snow, even when hungry, was majestic. Jacob knew this. Sometimes, during winter hunts, his father had not even raised his rifle to his shoulder when looking at a deer in the woods, quiet and gentle and graceful in its movements. He hoped not to see one, because he was not sure he could bring himself to shoot at it. And if he wasted a hunting trip, he could die.

But he did not see one this time; he saw only a rabbit. It was slow and awkward in the snow. Jacob wondered how it had survived the blizzard, whether it was buried and dug itself out or had some other, better survival mechanism that not even his own father had. *It was buried*, he assured himself. *It dug itself out.* He saw it when it was yards and yards away, farther than he would be able to shoot accurately, so he trudged after it through the snow—and on top of the crust that had formed on it, when it was thick enough. He followed it carefully, so as not to scare it off. It scampered across the snow, picked at the thin branches of half-buried saplings and the bark strips of birch trees. For hours Jacob watched it move between trees, always staying close to trunks. Whenever it stopped, he moved five feet closer, then walked with it to the next tree, then five feet closer. He did this while the sun fell from its low perch to its lower bed, and soon there was not much light to see by.

He positioned himself so he was on its side when it stopped, like his father told him to be, and he aimed at the head. The eye: he was not afraid to look there. It was black and dull, since there was so little light. He shot. The rabbit jerked. He approached it, feeling a sense of revenge, and picked it up by its hind legs. He watched the blood splat on the snow. Its fur was patchy and poorly colored, and its ears had nips and scratches all up and down them. It was an old rabbit, but he still wanted it. It made him realize how hungry he was, how little he had eaten in the days since his father died.

He ran back to the cabin and just beat sundown. Huffing, he set the rabbit on the wood-chopping stump and took out his knife. He sliced up its side like his father showed him. It steamed, and he had the urge, again, to slide his hands in the animal's warmth. He did, and in its heat he imagined his mother and father were back, ready to congratulate him on a good hunt, for providing for them all. Jacob gently scooped the rabbit's guts, then made only two slices and pulled away all the organs. He poked through it to make sure he had cut the vestigius out without bursting it. And there it was. He squished it between his fingers, threw it as far as he could, kept the liver and the heart, set the rest on the stump. He then skinned and butchered the rabbit and set the meat on the stove inside.

He ate it. It was not enough; the rabbit was small and weakened by the cold. He cooked the liver and ate it, too, and then the heart. He dwelled on the heart, savoring its heaviness, its toughness, the way it made him work to eat it. When he finished, he was still hungry. But there was nothing to be done.

◊

Six days after his father was buried, it was time to take the rabbit hide out of the tanner. He used the tongs again, and gloves, and squeezed the liquid out of the hide. Then he draped it over the line again, and dumped the extra tanner outside. It melted a patch of the snow into a pit and turned the edges an ever-so-slight shade of pink. He took the hide down and washed it gently with detergent, then rinsed it in another bucket and squeezed it dry. He hung it up again. It would hang for two more days before it was fully dry, before it was time to work it, make it soft. Then he would make it into a hat. Or lining for his boots. Or maybe something else entirely. He had not decided.

◊

Mr. Marks kept his word; he visited regularly. The path was long and winding, and his boots were not made for the woods, so he arrived blue-lipped and shivering. The length of his trips required him to stay overnight. On these nights, Jacob let him sleep in the bed that once belonged to him; he took his father's.

On his second visit, Mr. Marks commented on the empty cupboard shelves.

"I was just going hunting," Jacob said, picking up his gun, although he was too tired to hunt. He did not like Mr. Marks, resented his coming and going as if he held some authority over Jacob, as if he could see that there was no food and thus be justified in taking him away to a home for boys like him who were not smart enough to get rid of the people who pestered them. He understood now why his father argued with Mr. Marks all those times.

Except he didn't understand.

From the doorway, he turned back to Mr. Marks. "How did you know Daddy?"

"He was my best supplier," Mr. Marks said. He smiled.

"How else?"

"That's all."

Jacob stood. He wanted more.

Mr. Marks smiled. He looked at the photograph of Jacob's mother over the fireplace. "We had a mutual acquaintance."

Jacob nodded. The photograph had not been dusted since the last time his father did it. He would do it later, he thought, and went out into the cold.

◇

He shot another rabbit. It was bitter out, though, and the wind blew harder than it had since the storm that killed his father. He did not have his rabbit-fur hat—he forgot it in his hurry out of the cabin—and so he was shivering before he even made it out of the clearing. By the time he made it back, he could barely see for the cold that consumed him, and was barely aware of himself. The sun was setting quickly.

Mr. Marks met him at the door and took the rabbit from him. "Sit by the fire," he said, "and I'll take care of this." Jacob did, and slowly he returned to himself so that he knew where he was and what was happening.

"It was cold," he said. "Out there."

"It is cold," said Mr. Marks. He was slicing up the rabbit clumsily, Jacob could see. For a leather man, he was unskilled with skin and flesh. Soon, the table was shiny with blood.

"I can do it," he told Mr. Marks.

"No, no, I'm just out of practice."

Jacob dozed by the fire while Mr. Marks finished and set the meat on the stove to cook. When he awoke, there was a bowl on his lap, steaming.

"Eat up."

He did. He fell asleep.

◇

It was still dark when he awoke. The fire still burned brightly somehow, though it needed more wood. The air around the hearth waved softly from the heat. Mr. Marks was gone. The rest of the rabbit was gone, too. Likely so Mr. Marks would not be ashamed of his poor butchering.

Everything was silent. But something was wrong.

He stoked the fire first and then walked around the cabin, looking through each window as he passed it, throwing the latch over the door when he got there. He took his rifle down from the wall and paced. There was something happening. The air, or something, felt wrong.

Him. It was he. He felt wrong. The realization came slowly, starting as a soft twitch in his side. It turned into a stitch, and then a cramp, and then a pain that made him double over to try to relieve it. It was his stomach, not his muscles; something inside him, something he had eaten, something Mr. Marks had fed him. He clutched his stomach and heaved, pounded on it, gagged himself with his finger, but it all stayed down. The night swirled around him; he felt heavy and light at the same time, and fell into a heap on the floor. He caught glimpses of things as he twisted against himself: the pelt hanging in the corner, the small pile of skins he had cut but not treated before they turned sour, the frosted window. There were shapes in the window—round, maybe, and dark—and on those shapes, more shapes. He closed his eyes tight— he could not keep them open anymore—and he saw the shapes more clearly, pieced them together to make something he could identify. A face. Of course. He knew without thinking that it was the Bunnyman, and that it would kill him, was already killing him, somehow. He would not avenge his mother and father, he would not hunt down this creature and flay him with his own knife, the knife his father had taught him to hold and to sharpen and to wield. He would not parade the corpse of the Bunnyman through the streets of the town on an ox-drawn cart, triumphant and heroic. The Bunnyman would come inside, slit him here on the floor. There would be blood and pain and gore, and no one to find him like he had found his father.

Other than Mr. Marks, perhaps. But Jacob hated him, and he deserved that.

He braced himself for the slice across his chest. He arched his back, involuntarily at first, and then because he knew the claws could cut him more cleanly if he lay that way, his skin taut, without tearing him, and he dug his fingers into the floor beneath him, scratched violently at the oak boards, and his fingers went numb from the cold radiating up from the frozen earth, through the snow, through the wood of his great-grandfather's cabin. His fingers went first, then his toes, his hands, his lips, his tongue, his eyes; everything numb, and cold, and as much as Jacob could know anything as he lay there, writhing, he knew that a fire still burned.

Untitled

Jennifer Reimer

You can see this splitting from any distance. The water a distant memory across the cracked flats, all the dead tipped sideways on the seafloor. Our skin breathes through fog, through warm clothes and any number of echoes. Say anything, say this tide pool is nothing but our blood. Forget about saving the earth. We are collecting seawater. We write in the sand with a series of broken shells.

Untitled

Jennifer Reimer

Because there is more faith there is more blood. We count more stars in the sky yet altitude exhausts us. From time to time we wish that there were not so many points of light, so many wild places. Silence is the glass we look through when we apprehend each other. I have repaired the nets and broken the husks off rice but we have lost our way around 'cast' and 'mouth.' You say we've arrived where things fall apart and then come back together. You say this looks and feels like what it is—the start of a country at the end of the world.

Contributors.

◊**Jacob M. Appel** has published short stories and essays in more than one hundred fifty literary journals, most recently in *Conjunctions, Gettysburg Review,* and *Saranac Review.* He is a graduate of the MFA program in fiction at New York University, teaches at the Gotham Writers' Workshop and practices medicine at The Mount Sinai Hospital. More at: www.jacobmappel.com. ◊**Lisa Badner** has published poems in *TriQuarterly, Mudlark,* and forthcoming in *The Cape Rock.* She is a lawyer and lives in Brooklyn, NY. Lisa is a student in the Master Class at The Writers Studio. ◊**Matthew S. Baker** is a recent graduate of the MFA program at Virginia Commonwealth University, where he served as the 2008-2009 Associate Editor for *Blackbird: an online journal of literature and the arts.* ◊**Jason Bayani** is a recent graduate of Saint Mary's MFA program. He is a Kundiman fellow and a highly regarded veteran of the National Poetry Slam scene. He co-founded the Pilipino American poetry collective, Proletariat Bronze and has toured across the country, reading his work. He currently teaches at Saint Mary's. ◊**Karina Borowicz** has recent work in *Rattle, New Ohio Review,* and *MiPOesias.* Her translations have appeared on *Poetry Daily.* She lives in western Massachusetts. ◊**Michael Reid Busk** is a PhD student in the University of Southern California's Literature and Creative Writing Program. His work appears or is forthcoming in *Gettysburg Review, Florida Review, Fiction International,* and other journals. ◊**Maxine Chernoff** chairs the Creative Writing Department at SFSU and is editor of *New American Writing.* She is the author of six collections of fiction and ten books of poetry, most recently *The Turning* (Apogee Press, 2009). Her co-translation of *The Selected Works of Friedrich Hoelderlin* won the 2009 PEN America Translation Award. She taught in Prague in the summer of 2010. ◊**Jackie Corley's** short story collection, *The Suburban Swindle,* was released in October 2008 by So New. She publishes *Word Riot,* an online literary magazine and small press available at wordriot.org. "Fine Creature" is an excerpt from a novel in progress. ◊**KC Eib** received a BA in Theatre from Missouri State University. For a number of years he performed, directed, and adapted original material for community theatres based in Kansas City. Most recently, he received an MFA in Creative Writing from The University of Alaska Fairbanks. His work has appeared in *Alaska Quarterly Review.* He currently resides in Bremerton, Washington. ◊**Steve Gronert Ellerhoff** is an Iowan. He holds an MA in Creative Writing from Lancaster University in the UK and spent five years as the Director of Wind-Up Toys at Finnegan's Toys & Gifts in Portland, Oregon. Currently he is pursuing an MPhil in Literature of the Americas at Trinity College Dublin. ◊**Stephen Elliott** is the author of seven books including *The Adderall Diaries.* He usually sends an email to The Daily Rumpus list five times a week. ◊**Renee Emerson's** writing has appeared or is forthcoming in *The American Literary Review, Big Muddy, Reed Magazine,* and other publications. Her chapbook is *Something Like Flight* (Sargent Press, 2010). She holds an MFA from Boston University, and lives in Kentucky with her husband. ◊**Noah Gershman's** apartment was let to the girl from Cincinnati. Then Gershman crossed the continent of Africa by car. ◊**Jenny Hanning** lives in Texas. Her stories and poetry have been included in *Ninth Letter, Quarterly West, Post Road* and others. ◊**Peter Harris** teaches American Literature and poetry writing at Colby College in Maine, where he is the Zacamy Professor in English. He has published numerous articles on contemporary American poetry and a chapbook, *Blue Hallelujahs.* His poetry has appeared in many magazines including *The Atlantic Monthly , Epoch, Prairie Schooner, Ploughshares, Rattle, Seattle Review,* and *Sewanee Review.* A former Dibner Fellow, he has been awarded residencies at Macdowell, the Guthrie Center, Red Cinder House, and The Virginia Center for the Creative Arts. Harris has also taught at Marie Curie University in Lublin, Poland, and at University College Cork. He is a Zen Buddhist priest. ◊**Jane Hilberry** is a Professor of English at Colorado College, where she has taught Creative Writing for twenty years. Jane' s book of poems *Body Painting* (Red Hen Press) won the 2005 Colorado Book Award for Poetry. Her poems have appeared in many magazines, including T*he Hudson Review, Denver Quarterly,* and *The Women's Review of Books.* Her most recent book of poems is a collaboration with her father, poet Conrad Hilberry, titled *This Awkward Art: Poems by a Father and Daughter* (Mayapple Press 2009). She also edited the recently published volume *The Burden of the Beholder: Dave Armstrong* and *The Art of Collage* (The Press at Colorado College 2010) ◊**Adam Johnson** is a former Wallace Stegner Fellow and the Senior Jones Lecturer in Creative Writing at Stanford University. Winner of the Whiting Writers' Award, the Gina Berriault Award, and an NEA Fellowship, he is the author of a short story collection *Emporium* (2002), and the novel *Parasites Like Us* (2003) which won the California Book Award. His fiction has appeared in *Esquire, Harper's, The Paris Review, Tin House* and *Best American Short Stories.* The excerpt that appears here is from his recently completed novel, tentatively titled *The Orphan Master's Son.* ◊**Kasper Hauser** is a San Francisco-based sketch comedy group comprised of **Rob Baedeker, James Reichmuth, John Reichmuth** and **Dan Klein**, co-authors of *Obama's Blackberry, Weddings of the Times,* and *SkyMaul: Happy Crap You Can Buy from a Plane.* ◊**Myron Michael** is a recording artist, writing teacher, Cave Canem Fellowship recipient, and proprietor of Rondeau Records. His words appear online and in *The Harvard Review, Days I Moved Through Ordinary Sounds* (City Lights, 2009), *Tea Party,* and *Nanomajority.* He is the author of *Scatter Plot* (chapbook, forthcoming), and co-author of *Hang Man* (Move Or Die, 2010). ◊**Dan Moreau's** work appears in *Redivider, Portland Review,* and *Los Angeles Review.* His work has been nominated for a Pushcart Prize and received a grant from the Elizabeth George Foundation. He lives in Chicago. ◊**James O'Brien** has attended Iowa State University's MFA Program in Creative Writing and Environment since Fall 2008. He writes fiction and teaches advanced composition. His work has appeared in *NY Tyrant, J Journal, Portland Review,* and *Pisgah Review.* O'Brien is currently at work on a collection of short stories and a novel. ◊**Charlotte Pence** is a Ph.D. candidate in Creative Writing at the University of Tennessee and the former editor of *Grist.* She has received a fellowship from the Tennessee Arts Commission, a New Millennium Writing award, and most recently, the Discovered Voices 2009 Award. Her work has appeared or is forthcoming in *North American Review, Prairie Schooner, Denver Quarterly, Kenyon Review Online, Tar River, Iron Horse*, and many other journals. Weekly, she reviews a contemporary poem or song on her blog: www.charlottepence.blogspot.com ◊**Alice Pero** is a New Yorker, who somewhat reluctantly became a left-coaster in 1996. She lives in Los Angeles with her husband and no cats. Her book, *Thawed Stars* was praised by Kenneth Koch as having "clarity and surprises." She runs the celebrated reading series, Moonday, in Pacific Palisades, CA. ◊**Molly Prentiss** recently received her MFA in Creative Writing at the California College of the Arts and is now a resident writer at Workspace with the Lower Manhattan Cultural Council. She has been published in *La Petit Zine, Miracle Monacle, Plaid Review, The City Reader,* and elsewhere. She is a co-director of an arts and writing collective called factorycompany, that works to make more room for making. Her writings and drawings can be found at mollyprentiss.blogspot.com ◊**Jennifer A. Reimer** has an MFA in Writing from the University of San Francisco. Her poetry and fiction have appeared in *Our Stories, The Denver Quarterly, The Berkeley Poetry Review, The Chaffey Review, 580 Split, Tinfish, Puerto del Sol, Zoland* (forthcoming), and *Weave* (forthcoming). She's currently a graduate student in Comparative Ethnic Studies at the University of CA, Berkeley. She's the co-founder of Achiote Press. ◊**Ann Robinson** grew up on a farm in Arkansas and owns a farm there. She worked in the Traffic and Criminal Department in Marin County for 24 years. She is published in *American Literary Review, California Quarterly, Connecticut Review, The New York Quarterly, Poet Lore, River Sedge,* and *Spoon River Review*. ◊**Elizabeth Robinson** is the author of several books of poetry including *Apprehend, Apostrophe,* and the more recent *The Orphan & its Relations* and *Also Known As*. Robinson has been a recipient of the National Poetry Series, The Fence Modern Poets Prize and a grant from the Foundation for Contemporary Arts. She lives in Boulder, Colorado and is a co-editor of EtherDome Chapbooks and Instance Press. ◊**Michael Schiavo** is editor of *The*

Equalizer. His ranges have appeared in *Forklift, Ohio, The Normal School, La Petite Zine, Cold-Drill, jubilat, The Awl, Sixth Finch,* and *We Are So Happy To Know Something.* He lives in Vermont. ◊**Dawn Tefft** is a PhD student in Creative Writing at UW-Milwaukee. Recent publications include poems in *Witness, Third Coast,* and *Court Green.* Her poem "In the House of the House of Miniatures" was nominated for a Pushcart by *Witness.* Her e-chapbook, *Field Trip to My Mother and Other Exotic Locations,* can be found at *Mudlark.*

The Editors would like to thank the following bookstores for carrying *Fourteen Hills*:

In the Bay Area:
Adobe Books
Aardvark Books
Alexander Books Co.
Analog Books
Bird and Becket
Book Zoo
Books and Bookshelves
Books, Inc.
Booksmith
Bound Together Books
Canetti's Bookshop
Christopher's Books
City Lights
Cover to Cover
Diesel Bookstore
Dog Eared Books
Eastwind Books Berkeley
Farley's
Green Apple
Issues
Main Street Cafe and Books
Modern Times
Needles & Pens
Pegasus and Pendragon
Phoenix Books
SFSU Bookstore
Smoke Signals
University Press Books
USF Bookstore
Walden Pond Books
West Portal Bookshop

In California:
Avid Reader :: Sacramento
Bookstore Benicia :: Benicia
Bookshop Santa Cruz :: Santa Cruz

Captiola Book Cafe :: Santa Cruz
Copperfield's Books :: Petaluma
Kepler's :: Menlo Park
Main Street Books :: Los Altos
Orinda Books :: Orinda
Reader's Books :: Sonoma
Sawyer's News :: Santa Rosa
Watershed Books :: Lakeport
William Jessup University :: Rocklin

Across the U.S.:
57th Street Bookstore :: Chicago, IL
Atomic Books :: Baltimore, MD
Avril 50 :: Philidelphia, PA
Book Corner :: Bloomington, IN
Chicago Main Newsstand :: Evanston, IL
Crescent Tobacco Shop :: Tucson, AZ
Hudson News Grand Central :: NY, NY
Ink On A :: NY, NY
Magazine Cafe :: NY, NY
Magpies Newstand Cafe :: Durango, CO
McNally Jackson Books :: NY, NY
Newsbreak Swansea :: Swansea, MA
Newsland Alburquerque :: Alburquerque, NM
Nick Smoke Magazine :: NY, NY
Paras News :: NY, NY
Praire Lights :: Iowa City, IA
Quimby's Books :: Chicago, IL
Regulator Bookshop :: Durham, NC
Sam Weller's Zion Bookshop :: Salt Lake City, UT
St. Marks Books :: NY, NY
Tattered Cover Books Cherry Creek :: Denver, CO
Union Square Magazine Shop :: NY, NY
Universal News Broadway :: NY, NY
University Bookstore Wisconsin :: Madison, WI
Women and Children First :: Chicago, IL
Writer's Center :: Chicago, IL
Writer's Center :: Bethesda, MD

METONYM

WILLIAM JESSUP UNIVERSITY LITERARY JOURNAL

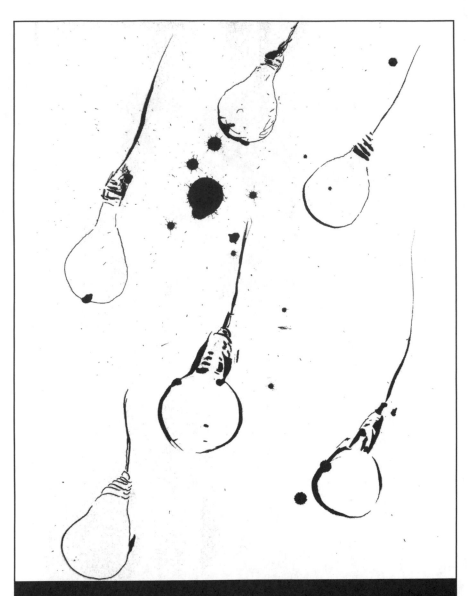

NOON

A LITERARY ANNUAL

1324 LEXINGTON AVENUE   PMB 298   NEW YORK   NEW YORK   10128

EDITION PRICE $12 DOMESTIC $17 FOREIGN

THE SOUTHEAST REVIEW

2011 Contests

World's Best Short-Short Story Contest $500

Judge: Robert Olen Butler

***Southeast Review* Poetry Contest $500**

Judge: David Kirby

***Southeast Review* Narrative Nonfiction Contest $500**

Judge: Mark Winegardner

Postmark deadline: March 15th, 2001. For more details visit southeastreview.org

A Publication of the
University of California:
Berkeley English
Undergraduate Association

The Folio is the UC Berkeley student-
run English undergradaute journal.
We publish the outstanding work of
undergraduates every spring.

Issues can be purchased for only $2.
Please see our website listed below for
more information on how to order.

Find us on Facebook!

www.ocf.berkeley.edu/~thefolio
thefolioucb@gmail.com

Superstition Review

The Online Literary Magazine
at Arizona State University

We are happy to announce the
launch of Issue 5 of Supersition Review,
online beginning late April 2010. Join us
online at **www.superstitionreview.com** to
view the works of the artists and writers
featured there this semester.

Our current and past issues include:

Adrian C. Louis, Barbara Kingsolver, Billy
Collins, Brian Doyle, Carol Ann Bassett, Cary
Holladay, Charlotte Holmes, Daniel Orozco,
Deborah Bogen, Edith Pearlman, Elizabeth
Searle, Jane Bernstein, Jesse Lee Kercheval,
Joan Connor, Kelli Russell Agodon, Leslie
Epstein, Michael S. Harper, Pam Houston,
Sherman Alexie, Sherril Jaffe and more!

An anthology commemorating Fourteen Hills' ongoing
dedication to innovative fiction.

Stephen Elliott, Peter Orner, Eireene Nealand, Pam Houston, Robert Glück
Nona Caspers, John Cleary, Pamela Ryder, and many more

Price (shipping and handling included): $15.00 Qty_____
Name_____
Street Address_____
City_____ State/Province_____
Zip/Postal Code_____ Country_____
Phone_____ E-mail_____

Also available on Amazon or from Small Press Distribution
www.spdbooks.org

Subscribe to Fourteen Hills

Please circle one. Prices include shipping and handling.

Single issue (current): $9

One Year (two issues): $15

Two Years (four issues): $28

Institutional (one year): $17

Back Issues (please specify): $5

Volume_____No._____Qty____

Name_____

Street Address_____

City_____ State/Province_____

Zip/ Postal code_____ Country_____

Phone_____ E-mail_____

Please enclose a check payable to Fourteen Hills: The SFSU Review and mail to :
Fourteen Hills
Department of Creative Writing
San Francisco State University
1600 Holloway Avenue
San Francisco, CA 94132-1722